Moving Beyond Your Past

Facilitator's Guide

TIM SLEDGE

Before I Said Goodbye Books
Houston, Texas

ISBN 978-0-578-52854-0 (Paperback)

Dewey Decimal Number 615.8
Subject Heading: Church Work with the Hurting\\ Dysfunctional Families

Sources for definitions in *Moving Beyond Your Past*:
By permission. From Merriam-Webster's Collegiate Dictionary, Tenth Edition ©1993 by Merriam-Webster Inc., publisher of the Merriam-Webster® dictionaries

Unless otherwise indicated, biblical quotations are from the Holy Bible, New International Version, copyright© 1973, 1978, 1984 by International Bible Society (NIV). Other versions used: the New American Standard Bible. © The Lockman Foundation, 1960, 1962, 1963, 1968, 1971, 1972, 1973, 1975, 1977. Used by permission; the King James Version (KJV).

Printed in the United States of America

Before I Said Goodbye Books
Houston, Texas
Tim Sledge, Publisher

http://www.TimSledge.com/ContactTimSledge.aspx

This group that you will lead is called a Heart-to-Heart group. During these 13 weeks the members of your group will share on Heart-to-Heart level as you discuss brokenness, surrender, and recovery.

Table of Contents

About the Author

Tim Sledge is a former Southern Baptist minister, speaker, and writer. Born and raised in West Texas and called to ministry at the age of 16, Sledge is a graduate of Billy Graham's alma mater, Wheaton College, and earned Master of Divinity and Doctor of Ministry degrees from Southwestern Baptist Theological Seminary in Fort Worth, Texas.

After devoting his career as an evangelical preacher to leading and growing ministries in Illinois, Tennessee, New Jersey, and Arizona, Sledge moved to a suburb of Houston, Texas, where he served as senior pastor of the Kingsland Baptist Church from 1985 to 1996. Under his leadership, the church's membership grew to more than 2000, with a growth in worship attendance four times the growth rate of the rapidly growing suburb where the church is located.

A key factor in the growth of Kingsland Baptist Church during those years was its support group ministry which began in the spring of 1988 when Sledge presented a sermon series on adult children of alcoholics. In the series, he talked about his experience of growing up with an alcoholic father and shared biblical, psychological, and personal insights for moving beyond a painful childhood. Support groups were offered during the series with participants using an interactive workbook that was based on the sermon topics. Over the next eight years, the congregation hosted 100 support groups and became known as "a healing place for hurting people."

The interactive workbook used in Kingsland's support groups evolved into the book *Making Peace with Your Past*. Originally published in 1992, *Making Peace with Your Past* has been translated in South Korea and Peru. *Making Peace with Your Past* and *Moving Beyond Your Past*, have been used as interactive workbooks for 20,000 support groups across the U.S.

Tim Sledge shares insights for inspiration and growth on his website: www.MovingTruths.com. Other books by Tim Sledge can be purchased on Amazon.com.

Introduction

A support group is composed of people who meet because of personal issues common to group members. Support groups focus on helping members gain awareness; understanding; and emotional, psychological, and spiritual support for dealing with personal life issues.

Moving Beyond Your Past is designed for use in lay-led support groups called Heart-to-Heart Support Groups. These are not therapy groups but are Christ-centered sharing groups that help people deal with issues related to their families of origin. *Making Peace with Your Past* is a recommended prerequisite to *Moving Beyond Your Past*.

Facilitating a Heart-to-Heart Group

Not every group leader is capable of facilitating a Heart-to-Heart Support Group. Special skills and experiences are required. If you have not led intensive support-group sessions before, read through the criteria for a facilitator on page 7.

Do not try to lead a *Moving Beyond* group until you have the training and skill necessary to lead such a group. If you do meet the criteria, the following material will help you prepare for your support group. Make prayer a major part of your preparation. God is deeply concerned about healing broken and hurting people.

Leading a Heart-to-Heart Group

Why Leading this Group Will Challenge You

In many ways facing the problems of the present is more difficult than is facing the pain of the past. Once we pass the first barriers of denial and shame about the past, we begin to feel more comfortable addressing it. After a while we begin to sense some power in confronting the past head on. The past is not a moving target, and you can develop a sense of having a grasp of your own past. Present problems, on the other hand, are moving targets.

One of the greatest challenges you will face in leading this group is an inclination on the part of the group members to discuss past pain rather than present issues. This will happen because members of your group still are dealing with the past. It also will occur because in some ways we can talk about the past more easily than we can the present. The past has happened. I can stand back and look at it, analyze it, and catalog it. I can learn to feel separate from it. In many ways I am the custodian of my past. I have great freedom to interpret it. I even may interpret some aspects of my past in a way that is most beneficial to me. I may ignore some things that I do not want to face.

When I deal with my present, others interpret it along with me. We cannot deal with the present as subjectively as we can the past. My compulsive behaviors have a way of becoming obvious when I most want to hide them. When I talk about pain in my past, I immediately begin to feel a power over it, but my present compulsions will not yield to me so easily.

Be prepared to keep pulling group members back to the present. You will need to talk about the past. At times you will need to do new probing into the past with group members. Remember that the challenge is always to bring the group member back to now. As facilitator you would ask the group member, "How is that affecting you now? What issues do you need to work on now?"

Some group members may feel that since they have completed their Face-to-Face group, they pretty much know everything about recovery. Gently but firmly help such group members look at present opportunities for growth. What present negative behaviors have roots in childhood experiences? In what areas do we still need to grow?

Some of the material in *Moving Beyond Your Past* is similar to material in *Making Peace with Your Past*. A group member may protest, "We've already covered this? Why do we keep going over the same ideas?" Our goal is not simply to be able to verbalize what a concept means. Our goal is to live out the truth of recovery concepts. For example, our goal is not to be able to say what boundaries mean; our goal is to exercise boundaries in our lives. Our goal is not simply knowing what denial is but stopping a pattern of living in denial. We do not want to merely name our compulsions; we want to stop them. Therefore, we will keep coming back to some elementary principles of recovery. As we recycle through different experiences of brokenness and surrender, we will utilize the same concepts over and over. Some people have compared this process to peeling an onion. You take off one layer at a time. Recovery means dealing with one layer of need at a time. You apply the concepts to one layer, then another, and then another. You use these concepts over and over. Group members need to learn all they can about these concepts because they can use them over and over for a lifetime.

This journey of emotional healing is like our spiritual walk. Sanctification is a day-by-day process of growth in which we are becoming more and more like Christ. Sanctification involves working on basic spiritual issues over and over and over. I need to keep working on my devotional life. I need to keep working on understanding the Bible. I never will live my spiritual life perfectly during this life. One day when I stand before Christ, He will make me just like Him. Until then, I am on a journey of spiritual growth.

For me emotional recovery is part of that journey. Jesus is concerned about the whole me, including my emotional life. Unresolved emotional problems hurt my spiritual growth. With the Holy Spirit's help I can tear down emotional barriers that keep me from being what God wants me to be. Sanctification is a journey. Emotional healing is a part of that journey—one aspect of the overall growth that God desires for me.

How do I think and speak of myself while I am on this journey? I must be honest with the fact that my compulsions always lurk close by waiting for an opportunity to overtake me, but in Christ I must not succumb to old labels that say I am just the same as I was at an earlier time.

In Christ I am saved. I am being saved. I will be saved. The same concept is appropriate for our emotional healing. I have been healed. I am being healed. I will be healed.

Knowing If You're Ready to Lead this Group

Group Facilitator Profile
A qualified Heart-to-Heart group facilitator—
1. Has completed a Face-to-Face group (or other intensive family-of-origin work) and has made positive changes in her life as a result of what she has learned;
2. Has made significant progress in understanding how her past has affected her present;
3. Has developed basic skills in experiencing and expressing his own emotions;
4. Has made significant progress in overcoming compulsive behaviors resulting from childhood issues;
5. Understands that emotional health and spiritual maturity are closely related;
6. Believes that spiritual growth is a long-term process and understands that people need time to grow;
7. Is continuing to grow emotionally and spiritually;
8. Has a growing relationship with Jesus Christ that guides his attitudes and values;
9. Has a good foundation of scriptural knowledge and is an active member of a local church;
10. Receives insight and support from other people;
11. Understands the danger of trying to fix people as opposed to letting them work through their own growth process with the help of God and others;
12. Knows how to lead a group without controlling it and can allow group members to experience and express their feelings;
13. Is willing to give time and energy to help members of the group.

Group Facilitator Support System
As a group facilitator you need someone to whom you can be accountable. You need support as you lead this group.

In our church support-group facilitators meet for dinner each week on a weeknight. We have found that meeting together each week before our groups meet is a great way to support each other. We discuss problems we face as we lead our groups. We share personal needs with each other. We are accountable to each other.

Don't depend on the group you lead as your only source of recovery work. You need some place where you are getting help for yourself. You may need to establish an ongoing relationship with a qualified Christian counselor. You will burn out if you do not have your own source of support.

Avoid working on your own issues while you are in the group leadership role. Share openly about struggles in your life, but don't look to your group to be the only place where you process these matters. Seek help from a qualified Christian counselor or share your personal issues with other facilitators.

Who Should Be in This Group?

A Typical Group Member Profile
The typical profile of a Heart-to-Heart group member—
1. Has completed a Face-to-Face group (or other intensive family-of-origin work);
2. Has developed a basic understanding of how his past has affected him;
3. Has begun learning how to experience his own emotions;
4. Has developed an ability to describe what she is feeling at a given time;
5. Has taken some positive steps in making changes in her life as a result of what she has learned;
6. Has demonstrated a desire for more emotional growth;
7. Is comfortable with the group process and knows how to interact in a group;
8. Is willing to work on present issues.

An Exception to the Profile
Some people cannot do much work in understanding the past until they have worked on the present. Certain addictions create such a break with reality that a person can do no meaningful emotional recovery work until he or she has a grasp of the addictive behavior and restores some contact with reality. Also, sometimes a person may need help immediately and a Heart-to-Heart group is all you have available.

For these reasons, on rare occasions some people can profit from working through this study before they study *Making Peace with Your Past*. The normal approach of a *Moving Beyond Your Past* support group (called a Heart-to-Heart group) is geared to people who already have done some work on understanding the impact that past experiences have had on them. If you admit to your group people who have done no previous recovery work, I suggest they number no more than one or two out of a group of six to eight individuals counting yourself.

Alumni from An Earlier Group?

You may have a cluster of group members who were in an earlier group together. This can be a strength for your group, but it can also be a problem. It can be a strength because these people already feel close to each other and find it easy to share with each other. It can be a problem if these group members focus more on each other than they do on members of the group who are new to them. You can alleviate this potential problem by bringing this issue out into the open at the first meeting. Encourage group members who have been in earlier groups together to focus consciously on connecting with group members whom they have not known previously. Be aware that differing levels of trust exist in the group. Work to help group members who already know and trust one another to develop trust with people who are new to them. Work on helping the new group members integrate fully into the group.

A Mixed Gender Group?

Mixed gender groups will work for this study. Men have much to learn from women, and women have much to learn from men. Women usually find it easier to be in touch with their emotions, and their example can help men get in touch with their own feelings while in the group. However, at this stage some advantages exist to same-sex groups. During this study group members will discuss their own compulsive behaviors. Women and men may be able to discuss such matters more freely in a same-gender group. Women's groups work well. Women can develop a tremendous network of support for one another within a women-only group. The same is true of men. Since 1992 I have led a men's support group in our church. This group has been one of the most powerful and most rewarding support-group experiences I have had. I have found that a group of men who have had some initial experiences in being open, in expressing their emotions, and in discussing their problems can set the example for other men who are new to the idea of openness and sharing. Men can share with other men at a deep level once they break through an initial layer of resistance.

If you lead a mixed group of people who already have been together in a Face-to-Face group, be especially careful about the danger of inappropriate relationships developing. When individuals share their second group together, a deep sense of camaraderie will exist. The level of emotional intimacy will be high. This closeness is not a bad thing, but it can make some people more vulnerable to inappropriate relationships. Problems can occur when a person feels more emotional closeness with the support group than with his or her spouse. This does not mean you never should have a mixed gender group. Inappropriate relationships can develop in any mixed group in the church. It means you need to help group members set and maintain boundaries. An inappropriate relationship might involve sexual behavior, or it simply could be a relationship in which a person works more diligently at emotional closeness with another group member or the opposite sex than with his or her spouse. Here are some ways you can help group members avoid inappropriate relationships.

1. Alert group members to the danger.
2. Ask that group members leave soon after each meeting is over. A man and woman staying on site for a prolonged conversation after a group meeting should not be considered acceptable.
3. Ask group members to report to the group on any developing relationships with other group members.
4. Ask group members to talk to you if they feel problems are developing with anyone in the group.
5. Ask group members to be willing to be confronted if you or another group member sense a problem developing.

Please do not be frightened by this warning. God wants us to learn to be emotionally intimate with other humans. Intimacy means honestly sharing with one another. Such sharing can occur in support groups in a positive way. People can set and maintain boundaries. Simply remember that you are working with people who may not have much experience with intimacy or with boundaries. They will need your help and guidance.

Finally, you as the group facilitator also need to be wary of the danger of inappropriate relationships. As you help group members, some will develop deep feelings of gratitude toward you. Some group members may develop strong feelings of closeness to you that they do not know how to express. Do not exploit such feelings. Maintain your role as group leader and friend, nothing more. Do not endanger the support-group ministry of your church by getting involved in an inappropriate relationship. One way to strengthen and protect yourself in this area is to develop your own support system which includes being accountable to someone.

Why The First Meeting Is Crucial

The primary goal of the first meeting is to experience group bonding. In a Face-to-Face group, this bonding occurs as group members tell something about childhood that is painful to remember and to discuss. Strong emotions, sharing of untold secrets, and instant bonding characterize the first meeting of a Face-to-Face group. Much of the emotional intensity of the first meeting of a Face-to-Face group grows out of the fact that many of the group members are openly discussing painful childhood issues with other people for the first time. Assuming that most or all of the members of your Heart-to-Heart group have already participated in a Face-to-Face group, you may not see the same level of intensity during the first meeting of your Heart-to-Heart group.

While the first meeting of your Heart-to-Heart group may not be as intense as was the first meeting of your Face-to-Face group, it still can be a powerful experience. The meeting guide for the first meeting lists discussion questions to help group members make a strong initial connection with one another.

Foundational Concepts

Moving Beyond Your Past is built on 10 foundational concepts:

CONCEPT 1: Making peace with your past is of limited value if you do not move beyond your past by changing present negative behaviors.

In one sense we continually deal with the past. New understanding of past events unfolds day by day. The process is like unpeeling layers of an onion. When a person begins the process of recovery, he or she takes giant steps. The recovering person embraces the past with all its pain and begins a new journey. As time passes he or she remains open to new insights from past experiences.

At some point the focus needs to shift from a backward focus to a present focus. While not closing themselves to insights from the past, group members must begin to look at present-tense issues. My past is affecting my present life. I now understand that more than ever. Now the question is, "What am I going to do about these present behaviors?" If I become an expert on understanding what happened to me in the past, but I still live a lifestyle filled with negative behaviors spawned by my painful past, I have some important work to do. Some individuals run from their past, then embrace it, but get stuck in it. Making peace with your past is a stage of a journey. It is not the whole journey.

CONCEPT 2: We often use compulsive behaviors to mask emotional pain.

All compulsive behavior has one thing in common: The emotional pain I try to avoid lessens when I am engaged in my compulsive behavior. In recovery I learn to feel my pain rather than run from it. Once I learn to experience my feelings as they occur and then move on, my compulsive behaviors are outdated. They no longer serve their original purpose.

CONCEPT 3: A compulsive behavior does not go away just because you learn why you started the behavior.

Emotional patterns are difficult to break. Learning to feel my emotions as they happen takes time. I may succeed at it about 90 percent of the time today and 20 percent of the time tomorrow. Breaking a life-long pattern of suppressing what I feel does not happen overnight. My compulsive behaviors still will serve me when I am running from my feelings. Letting go of my compulsions means letting go of a big security blanket.

Some compulsions develop a power outside the emotional cause. Even when I am doing very well at experiencing my feelings rather than running from them, I will find that my compulsive behaviors have a life of their own.

Even when I understand why I do what I do, these compulsions hold on to me with a death-defying grip. I not only must address the root of the compulsive behavior, I now must address the behavior itself, for it has developed a life of its own.

It may be a substance that carries its own addictive grip. It may be a behavior that continues by sheer force of habit.

CONCEPT 4: You are responsible for your behavior.

Many people see recovery as a way to avoid responsibility. "I can't help myself; My childhood made me this way," is what many people assume recovery advocates are saying. Recovery is based on the conviction that with God's help I can change.

Recovery is about understanding who I am and how I came to be the way I am so that with God's help I can change the way I am. Ultimately, recovery is about taking responsibility for my behavior now.

CONCEPT 5: To change the way you act, you must grow spiritually.

Those of us who grew up in difficult family situations vowed to get control of life. If things are not working, we simply will try harder. We vow to expend more and more effort to solve whatever problems we face.

Such thinking is not all bad, but when we seek to change how we live from day to day, effort is not enough. We need an inner spiritual change. We need a power beyond ourselves.

CONCEPT 6: Unaddressed emotional issues will hinder spiritual growth.

Unresolved emotional issues become barriers that block us from receiving the full impact of God's power. As we understand our emotional issues better, we can clear away these barriers. At some points our emotional insights open new spiritual vistas. At other points our spiritual insights open us to emotional healing.

CONCEPT 7: Emotional wholeness affects your relationships with self, others, and God.

Some people are "spiritual" but cannot relate to other people. Some people get along with others but secretly detest themselves. Some people have great self-understanding but lack spiritual depth. God desires wholeness and balance in our lives. Turning God loose in your life means letting Him work in all areas of your life.

CONCEPT 8: Spiritual and emotional growth occur in cycles.

We desire continual and uninterrupted growth. We want forward motion only. No setbacks. In reality we grow in cycles. The central concept of this study is that we grow in cycles of brokenness, surrender, and recovery. Once we understand this pattern as the norm, we can harness it for powerful growth.

CONCEPT 9: Support groups can provide a healthy atmosphere for spiritual and emotional growth.

A support group provides a tremendous environment to work on the cycles of recovery. For the support group to function well, certain elements must be present.

• **Group members must agree to a covenant**
Each person who participates in a Heart-to-Heart group must commit to the covenant listed below.

I AGREE to make attendance at all 13 group meetings a top priority. If I must be absent, I will miss no more than three meetings. If I miss more than three meetings, the group may decide whether I can continue in the group.

I AGREE to identify one or more compulsive behaviors and work on removing the behavior(s) from my life during the next 13 weeks.

I AGREE to be on time for each meeting. I recognize that I hurt myself and other group members when I am late.

I AGREE to stay until each meeting is adjourned. I recognize that I affect the dynamics of the group in a negative way if I leave early. My desire to leave early may be an expression of my unwillingness to face up to the feelings I am feeling in response to what is happening in the group. If I must leave the meeting early, I will explain my reasons to the group before I leave. I will be open to discussing my early departure at the next group meeting.

I AGREE that what takes place in the group is CONFIDENTIAL. If I break my commitment to confidentiality, I understand that I will be asked to leave the group.

(When you discuss the covenant with prospective group members, reserve the right to confer with a professional counselor, a staff supervisor, or your support-group leadership team about issues that come up in the group.)

I AGREE to do everything I can to help create an atmosphere of trust in the group.

I AGREE to be supportive of other group members as they struggle with their emotions. When needed I will encourage other group members with the words, "I support you."

I AGREE to engage in rigorous, not brutal, honesty toward myself and other group members.

I AGREE to be open to letting other group members confront me in love so that I can grow.

I AGREE to complete assigned homework so that I can grow and have meaningful interaction with group members during the group sharing times.

I understand that some sessions of the group may be emotionally intense. I AGREE to let my group leader know about any physical problems which might affect my participation in the group.

I AGREE to share with my group any developments in one-to-one relationships with other group members that occur outside the group meetings because relationships outside the group can hamper the group process.

(Note: This last part of the covenant is included to help group members avoid involvement in inappropriate relationships with each other. Also, even appropriate relationships which develop between group members outside the group's meetings can affect the dynamics of the group.)

This covenant is the way an individual expresses her initial commitment to the group. The covenant also helps a group member know what she can expect from other group members. The covenant is the cement that binds the group together before it experiences the closeness of sharing each other's stories and pain. The covenant sets the stage for the confidentiality that is crucial to the group's success. It alerts the potential group member that the group requires work outside of the group meetings. Each person who expresses an interest in the group should be asked to read the covenant. Anyone who is not willing to accept and sign the covenant should not be allowed to participate in the group.

• Group members need to give each other feedback
Feedback is an emotional mirror within the group which helps group members get in touch with their feelings and see themselves more objectively. Feedback can help group members be more honest with themselves about their own compulsive behaviors.

Feedback occurs when I tell you what I see and hear you saying. You may not be aware of the messages your facial expressions, body language, and even your words communicate. What is obvious to me as I watch and listen may be unknown to you, but by giving you feedback I can help you see what I see.

Feedback is nonjudgmental. When I give feedback I am not insisting that what I say is the way things are. I simply report what I see and hear. Through feedback group members begin to discover what reality is. At some point shutting out reality became a way of coping. A selective screening of reality became habitual. As I hear different group members giving me the same feedback, I can begin to see myself more objectively.

• Group members should help each other with boundaries
Boundaries are protective barriers which give us some control over how we live our lives and how other people relate to us. If someone tries to force sexual involvement on me, I have the right to say "No." That is a boundary.

Boundaries are not the same as walls. Walls shut people and feelings out. Walls keep me isolated from reality. Boundaries are flexible depending on the situation and the people involved. Boundaries are like filters. I let some things in. I keep some things out. I decide who gets close and who does not.

Our compulsive behaviors build walls around us. One of the challenges of the group is to help group members replace walls with boundaries. Group members can build new boundaries in their lives. Walls can be removed. Damaged boundaries can be repaired. Face-to-Face groups help group members begin the work of boundary repair. Heart-to-Heart groups continue the process.

Emotional boundaries protect against verbal abuse. Emotional boundaries set limits on manipulative behavior by others. Emotional boundaries remind me that I can feel my own feelings. I am not bound to feel the feelings of other people for them.

Physical boundaries include signals about where and when I will permit a particular person to touch me. Physical boundaries are about my right to protect myself from physical harm by others.

Sexual boundaries mean that I can say "No" to sexual advances. I have the right to set limits on what others do to me sexually. This may seem obvious to most people, but it may not be obvious to the victim of sexual abuse.

Spiritual boundaries. A healthy relationship with Jesus Christ is the only form of true religion. People can use religion, including some distorted expressions of the Christian faith, to manipulate and control through fear, shame, and guilt. Spiritual boundaries mean I can make choices about spiritual commitments. I do not have to be manipulated by people who seek to control my feelings and my life with twisted versions of religious truth. I can say "No" to people who attempt to portray God as unloving and unforgiving.

• Group members must support each other
Use the phrase "I support you" to encourage a group member when he gets stuck emotionally. Use the phrase "I support you" after a group member has shared something that is painful. Teach the members of your group to use this or a similar phrase. When your

group is functioning well, group members will offer words of encouragement spontaneously at different times throughout the meeting.

• Spouses should not be in the same group

If a husband and a wife participate in the same support group, several concerns are present.

- One of the two might not feel comfortable talking about his or her feelings and experiences in front of the other one.
- One spouse might be tempted to reinterpret the other's comments and feelings for the group. This would handicap the group process.
- When group members confront one spouse, the other spouse might try to defend him or her, thus interrupting the group process.

Some alternatives would be for one spouse to go through a group. The other partner then would participate in the next group offered. Another suggestion is that each spouse could be in a different group if the church offered two groups simultaneously.

In some cases the same concerns apply to two close friends. The two could be emotionally enmeshed to an extent that it would be impossible for them both to participate effectively in the same group.

CONCEPT 10: Surrender to God is the ultimate pathway to growth and healing.

Ultimately, recovery is about deepening one's commitment to Christ. The support group helps me to move past denial and to look at myself as I really am. What I see may be disheartening. I see myself as I really am, and I do not like what I see.

My need to change is so great that I realize I cannot do it by myself. I need help. I need the help of other people, but even that is not enough. I need God's help. I make myself available to His help through surrender.

One of the recurring daily assignments asks the members of the group to pray for one another by name. As group facilitator, give special attention to praying for specific needs of the members of your group. Each session will close with prayer. The closing prayer time is brief but powerful. Be careful not to use prayer as a substitute for talking through an emotional issue that your group members need to discuss. Be open to using prayer as a pathway to emotional healing.

Sometimes you will want to pray for a group member during a meeting. After you have helped the individual talk through his issues with the group, a focused prayer for a particular group member can be a powerful vehicle. Invite this person to sit in the center of the circle while each group member prays a simple prayer of petition and affirmation for him. This type of prayer is an effective way of lifting the individual's needs to God, and it allows the group to express support for this individual in a meaningful way.

Goals for a Heart-to-Heart Group

• **To move beyond the hurts of the past into joyful and productive day-to-day living**

In this group we want to focus on the present. Equipped with a knowledge of how the past affects present behaviors, we now begin our focus on changing the present behaviors that hurt us and that keep us from being all God wants us to be. We will continue to look into the past when doing so is necessary for understanding present behaviors, but our focus is on changing present behaviors.

• **To begin to experience freedom from compulsive behaviors**

Compulsive behaviors temporarily shield us from emotional pain rooted in the past. These behaviors develop their own strongholds in our lives apart from past emotional pain. Such harmful behaviors imprison us. In this study we challenge group members to focus on one or more compulsive behaviors they want to address. We will challenge members to report their progress in dealing with their particular compulsions.

• **To learn how to care for others without destroying yourself**

Caring for other people can be a way of avoiding a close look at who I am. Codependency is the name for helping others in a way that hurts me. It is another form of compulsive behavior. This kind of behavior is not about sacrificial Christian service. Such harmful behavior cripples my ability to care for myself in a way that enables me to give lasting help to others.

People who are codependent manipulate and control others as they care for them. In this study we will learn the difference between compulsive helping and Christlike caring.

• **To experience an atmosphere of trust, honesty, and unconditional love within the group**

An atmosphere of trust is crucial for a successful support group. Since your group will consist primarily of people who already have shared in a meaningful support-group experience, you will have a strong foundation on which to build. A major trust issue will be sharing personal struggles with compulsive behaviors.

Group members may feel shame about their compulsive behaviors. Being able to trust others with these present-tense struggles will be a step toward winning a victory over compulsive behaviors.

• **To encourage each group member to begin to take responsibility for his/her emotional and spiritual healing**

Ultimately each person can learn how to help himself or herself grow. This study is built on the concept of cycles of recovery. Understanding the cycles of recovery gives individuals a framework for lifelong growth. Recovery means moving beyond blaming and moving toward taking personal responsibility for growth.

• **To help group members be emotionally involved in what is happening in the group**

In the Face-to-Face group members learned to say, "This is what I am feeling, and this is why I am feeling this way." Group members will work on being connected with the emotional events in each meeting.

• **To develop spiritual vitality in the context of a commitment to Jesus Christ**

A painful past may leave you with ambivalent feelings about God. We will continue to examine ways in which painful past experiences affect our view of God. We will continue to work at breaking down emotional barriers which keep us from fully receiving God's love and grace. We will examine ways members can pursue further spiritual growth after they complete this group. Pages 203-204 in the *Moving Beyond Your Past* member's book contain suggestions for additional work.

• **To encourage group members to build on the discoveries they made in the Face-to-Face group**

In the Face-to-Face group, members learned to feel their feelings, to begin to trust others, to tell their stories even when it hurts, and to connect present behaviors with past pain. These experiences are foundational. In this study we will work from this foundation to gain new insights which will help us to change present negative behaviors.

Actions Basic to Effective Group Leadership

This section contains a list of actions basic to leading a Heart-to-Heart support group effectively. Each week we will ask you to work on some of the specific actions this section describes.

• Be Personally Involved without Relinquishing Leadership

Your role as group facilitator is not that of a trained expert who has solved all his or her problems and who shows up each week to help struggling group members with their problems. Your role is that of a fellow struggler—one who also understands struggling with compulsive behaviors and moving beyond emotional pain. At the same time, to lead effectively you must have reached a point of some success in dealing with the compulsive behaviors in your life.

You need to be emotionally vulnerable. Sharing some of your own emotional pain is crucial. However, you also must recognize that someone needs to be leading the group at all times. This means that you will not be able to move as deeply into personal sharing as a group member can.

From the first meeting of the group and even during the preliminary interviews with prospective group members, you will set the tone for the group meetings. If you model openness about your own struggles, the group will follow that example. If you display a condescending attitude, group members will have difficulty trusting and sharing.

Don't attempt to create emotions you don't feel or try to magnify your emotions to be a good example. The key is letting yourself get in touch with your feelings, and then being honest about them.

• Be Willing to Confront in Love

Sometimes love is tough. Sometimes caring for a person means being willing to say something to that person that he or she does not want to hear. The prevalence of denial in the lives of people who struggle with compulsive behaviors means that some confrontation will be necessary in your group. Confrontation motivated by love is sensitive to timing and wording. It is not hostile nor destructive. It is sensitive to how much the recipient can deal with at the time of the confrontation.

If you feel that you must smooth over or ignore every possible confrontation, you will have trouble leading this group. Confrontation is not always bad. It can lead to understanding and healing.

• Challenge Group Members to Keep Working on Their Compulsive Behaviors

Group members may want to focus on the past. They have learned to talk about their feelings now, and they may not want to talk about anything else. Challenge them to work on their compulsive behaviors. Remind them that they are in the group to change how they think and act.

• Communicate Acceptance and Concern

Shame is a big issue for people struggling with compulsive behaviors. In this group, you want to create an atmosphere that feels safe because it is safe—an atmosphere which communicates, "I accept you as you are." Accepting people as they are does not necessarily mean you agree with their values or choices. You can love a person without agreeing with that person. If a person's values need to change, a caring and sympathetic friend is more likely to impact those values than is a judgmental critic.

In the group you will hear people tell about things that make them feel ashamed. Sometimes the shame is irrational. It is about what someone else did, not about what the person who feels the shame did. Sometimes the shame will be appropriate. In either case, your role is not to make moral pronouncements but to support this person in love.

How do you communicate acceptance and concern? Here are some simple guidelines.

1. Listen intently and aggressively. When someone shares something that is emotionally painful, lean toward him or her. Use your facial expressions to show concern. Nod your head. When the person has to stop because the emotion is too strong, say, "I support you."

2. When a group member cries and says, "I'm sorry," say, "It's OK to cry in this group. We are here to share your pain."

3. Resist the temptation to make moral judgments every time a group member describes a situation you believe is wrong. This could make the group member feel that he could not share again safely. As you build a relationship with the person, you will have significant opportunities to influence moral choices later in the relationship. Do not interpret this as a lack of concern for moral values. It is a matter of strategy—of how you can get to the place of having a significant impact upon this person's life.

4. After a group member has shared something that makes her feel vulnerable and ashamed, say something like this, "I know that sharing what you just shared took a lot of courage. I admire you for being able to share it."

5. If a group member responds to another group member who has shared by condemning his actions or words, intervene. Remind the group that you are not here to judge each other.

• Create a Feeling of Safety in the Group

Group members need a safe place emotionally. Part of your role as group facilitator is to help create an atmosphere of safety and trust within the group. Here are some ways you can accomplish this goal:

1. Confidentiality
During the first meeting and during several subsequent meetings, remind the group of the importance of confidentiality. Kindly but firmly remind the group that anyone who breaks the commitment to confidentiality will be asked to leave the group. Reaffirm your commitment to confidentiality.

Remind the group that even telling someone else's story without using names can violate confidence. You inadvertently may share with the one person who can put the pieces together and determine who the story is about.

When you discuss the covenant with prospective group members, reserve the right to confer with a professional counselor, a staff supervisor, or the support-group ministry leadership team regarding issues that come up in the group. Make this clear before the group starts.

2. Confidence
As you lead the group, you will have times when you believe that you do not know what you are doing.

Remember to lean on God's direction and follow the instincts He gives you. You will make mistakes. The best leaders do.

You want to be honest about your personal struggles and open to the comments that group members make about your leadership. At the same time, starting with the first contacts you have with group members, you should convey an attitude of confidence.

Through your attitude and words, communicate, "This group will be a positive experience. It will provide much help to the people who participate in it. I feel that God has called me to lead this group, and it will work!"

Learn to distinguish the difference between openness, vulnerability, and humility on the one hand and a lack of self-confidence as a facilitator on the other hand. You want the former but not the latter.

3. Privacy
The group needs a sense of privacy about what it is doing. This starts with your choice of an appropriate meeting place. How you talk about the group in public affects this sense of privacy. Give group members a sense that you are committed to keeping what happens in the group a private matter.

4. Boundaries
As group facilitator, you will enforce certain boundaries during the meetings. You will not permit a group member to act in a verbally abusive way toward another group member. You will not force group members to do or say anything they are not willing to do or say. You will learn how to gently nudge a group member to a point of discovery and growth instead of using manipulation which pushes the individual group member to a place where she does not want to be.

5. Christian Identity
The direction the group takes should honor Christ and His Word. Many of the people who participate in your group will attend because it is a Christian group sponsored by a church. They especially need to hear you make a clear connection between what the group is doing and your personal faith in Christ. They may fear that the group work they are doing somehow violates their faith. They may have heard that all recovery work is associated with the New Age movement or some kind of secular psychology.

6. Facilitate Feedback
Read again on page 12 of this guide the material on the purpose and technique of feedback in a group. Your

role is to facilitate this type of feedback. Hopefully, members of your group already have some feedback skills. Set the example, and give them some room to follow your example. Let them learn that you will not always be the first one to speak. Watch the faces of group members as they listen to someone else share. If you see strong emotion in facial expressions or other body language, ask that person if he is willing to give some feedback.

• Help Group Members Connect the Past with the Present

Pain from the past affects present behavior. Sharpen your ability to see connections. Watch for things that don't add up. Pick up on feelings. Ask probing questions. Help group members to see how their compulsive behaviors connect with painful experiences from the past. For example you might ask someone who has shared that he has a problem with an addiction to food, "When is the first time you can remember eating to make yourself feel better emotionally?" or "Where did you enjoy eating when you were a child? What was special about this place?" The answers to questions like these could be a springboard to understanding the significance of food in this person's life now.

• Help Group Members Identify What They Are Feeling

Identifying emotions is important in this study because people often use compulsive behaviors to mask emotional pain. During the meetings help group members get in touch with their feelings. When you observe intense emotions in a particular group member, help the group member to name the emotions that are occurring. A good question to ask is, "Do you ever engage in compulsive behavior to deal with this emotion?" To help them bring concreteness to their behavior, you may ask them, if they are willing, to describe such an occasion.

• Help Group Members Understand Psychological Expressions of Biblical Truth

Moving Beyond Your Past places emphasis on helping people experience emotional maturity as they grow spiritually. This is accomplished by helping group members arrive at a psychological understanding of themselves within the context of biblical truth.

Our emotional health affects our spiritual health. Our spiritual maturity is not complete without emotional maturity. Beware of people who appear spiritually "mature" but who are emotionally ill. Emotional maturity is empty without spiritual maturity. Beware of a person who professes emotional maturity but who lives within a spiritual vacuum.

Sometimes people use religious "talk" to avoid facing emotional problems. Sometimes people do not meet their spiritual needs while they carefully address emotional issues.

As a facilitator, be very careful about using spiritual statements to manipulate group members. An example would be prefacing a statement with "God is telling me to tell you...." Assume that if God is leading you in what you are saying, the people who receive your message will sense God's presence in what you say.

• Know How to Start a Meeting

Arrive at the meeting place early. Greet group members as they arrive. Attempt to pick up on any feelings you sense in members as they arrive. Be careful to start the meeting when it is scheduled to start.

Begin by inviting group members to check in. Checking in means giving a brief report which could focus on any one of several areas:
1. What am I feeling emotionally now—anger, fear, guilt, joy, loneliness, sadness, shame?
2. How do I feel about the group process?
3. Is any pressing emotional or spiritual issue present that needs to be dealt with immediately?
4. What is my initial reaction to the material we studied this week?
5. How well have I managed my compulsive behaviors since the last group meeting?

For example you could start the checking-in time by asking, "Does anyone have anything pressing which you need to share today?" Or, "What happened in your life this last week as a result of something we discussed at last week's meeting?" The study material for the week or something which happened since the last group meeting may raise intense issues. A group member may need to talk about such an issue as soon as the group begins. Be willing to start the group meeting by responding to any pressing issue that group members raise during the initial period of checking in.

The first issue that members raise can lead into other issues that other group members voice. What one person shares will push certain buttons in the lives of other group members. They will describe their issues and you can lead the group to respond to them.

• Know How to Close a Meeting

You face two dangers in closing a meeting. One danger is that you always close the meeting at a specific time in response to a rigid schedule. If you operate this way you may close the meeting at the very point where a group member finally has gotten in touch with a significant issue and is ready to share. The group member will not necessarily be at the same point of readiness when you start the next meeting.

If you continue the meeting too long, some group members will become tired and frustrated. Spouses of group members may begin to have questions about the group. Learn to be flexible about the time of closing the meeting, but do not consistently end the meeting an hour later than the target time for adjourning. A group meeting can last from two to two and one-half hours.

About 30 minutes before you are ready to close the meeting, help the person on whom you are focusing reach a point of closure. Then ask, "Does anyone else have anything you need to talk about?" Take some time to respond to issues group members raise in response to your question. At some point cut off the discussion. Affirm the importance of what people are saying. Offer to pick up with the same topic next time. Ask the group member on whom you focused last to introduce the topic at the beginning of the next meeting.

Be sure you have tied up loose ends. Did you put someone on hold during the meeting? Did you ever get back to him? Was someone interrupted in sharing as you moved to focus on someone's response to her? Did you get closure with the original speaker?

Finally, ask group members to stand and join hands. Ask each group member to say a short prayer. Ask each group member to pray about "something that happened to me in this meeting that I am thankful for" or "a problem I am working on." Encourage group members to pray for themselves. This is an important part of learning to take care of oneself. Group members also may want to pray for each other. Encourage prayer for each other, but as a general rule keep the prayer time relatively brief.

Some group members may be reluctant to pray aloud. Tell the group members that if any of them do not want to pray aloud, that person simply should say "Amen," when it is her turn to pray. Don't make this too easy. This can be a good time for group members to become more comfortable with praying aloud. In some units we will make other specific suggestions for the closing prayer. After the closing prayer, the meeting is over. Do not restart the meeting after the closing prayer.

• Keep One Person from Dominating the Group

A characteristic of support groups is that each person has time to talk. Remove any sense of hurriedness. However, some people will talk too long.

When a person is going into too much detail and is losing the attention of the group, get things back on course. When this occurs you usually will notice that the person sharing is emotionally disengaged and that the group has disconnected. Discreetly interrupt the person who has talked too long. One way is to jump in and restate what you have heard. You might say, "So, what you are saying is...."

Another way is to interrupt and restate the question you asked originally. You might say, "(Name), what is causing you to keep engaging in this destructive behavior?" The speaker may be somewhat unsettled by this response, but he or she should respond by restating the response more succinctly. Still another method is to interrupt and ask the person if he or she would mind getting some feedback from the group.

• Read Nonverbal Communication

As group leader, you can grow by becoming a student of nonverbal communication. The group members will express nonverbally much of what is happening to them as they respond to the content of the meeting.

Here are some things to look for:

1. Posture and Body Orientation
How is an individual sitting in relation to the rest of the group? Is he turning outward as if he would like to face the other way? Is she leaning forward and listening intently? Does she communicate interest and involvement?

2. Facial Signals
Learn to read faces. Scan the group as a group member shares a painful incident from childhood. Look for

signs of intense emotional involvement. Depend on God for sensitivity. Do you see a face that is full of pain? Is someone holding back tears?

What messages do each group member's face convey? Fear? Intense thought? Do you perceive that this group member has shut down all or certain emotions?

3. Breathing Patterns, Gulps, Sighs

Listen for sighs, deep breaths, gulps. Think about the timing of these body responses. What do they mean? Ask questions.

• Stay Ready for Anything

Don't try to predict or anticipate everything that will happen in a group meeting. Some of the most significant things that will happen will not be planned and may not be related clearly to your agenda or the topic for the week. If you are a person who needs everything planned out, work on being spontaneous during the group meetings. Not knowing what will happen can produce some fear. Trust God to help you no matter what happens.

• Teach Group Members to Help Each Other

As the group progresses you will encourage group members to do more and more of the work in helping one another. You will model certain ways of responding and relating. Members will learn from you. After a few meetings you should not be the only one asking, "What are you feeling right now?" or saying, "I support you." Other group members can volunteer insights after they listen to a person share. As the group members catch on to these concepts, you will find yourself saying less and less.

• Utilize Good Listening Skills

Another aspect of your leadership role is aggressive listening. Much of your listening will be in the form of visual listening and watching for nonverbal cues. Listen carefully and store what you hear. You might want to make some notes after each meeting to help you remember what various group members shared. (Except for the first meeting, do not take notes during a meeting.) Some of the most effective help you will give will occur when you help a group member relate something he just said to something he said a few weeks ago.

• Validate Feelings

Remember that sharing emotions is difficult for members of your group. When a group member shares an emotion, commend her for sharing. Use statements like, "I know it must have been difficult for you to share that. Thank you for exercising the courage to share."

Jim may weep convulsively and then apologize. A good response would be asking several group members, "How do you feel about Jim's crying? Does it make you respect him less?" You will know which group members to ask, and you can expect them to respond with words like, "I admire someone who can let his emotions out. I support Jim for being able to cry."

Avoid telling a person that he is feeling the wrong thing or that a person is wrong for having a certain feeling. Your group will contain people who have trouble even finding their feelings. Once they find a feeling, they need help in learning how to name the feeling and in deciding how to respond to it. After they develop these skills, they will be ready for learning more about how to relate to people in a manner that lessens the likelihood of destructive feelings.

• Visiting Secular Groups for Insights

Visiting a secular 12-Step group can help as you prepare to lead a Heart-to-Heart group. You may not agree with everything you see and hear in a secular group. However, you will observe firsthand some procedures and concepts which will help you.

Look under Alcoholics Anonymous in your local phone book to start your search for groups like Adult Children of Alcoholics, Overeaters Anonymous, and Codependents Anonymous. Your phone book should contain a number you can call for more information.

One difference you will notice in most of these groups is that group members do not give feedback to one another. In the Heart-to-Heart group, group members give feedback to one another following the direction of the facilitator.

If your church does not have a support-group ministry, you also may want to consult churches in your area that have such ministries under way. Talk with the church's support-group coordinator to gain insights.

• Be Ready for Challenging Situations

1. What if Someone Quits the Group?
In a Face-to-Face group, members may drop out because facing unresolved childhood issues is too frightening to them. The likelihood of dropouts is less in a Heart-to-Heart group.

The people in your Heart-to-Heart group will be people who already have done some work on family-of-origin issues. They have taken the first frightening steps of the journey. However, facing compulsive behaviors is painful too, and as people face compulsive behaviors, other issues from the past may surface.

Sometimes people do drop out of groups. If someone quits the group, use some time in the following meeting to let the group talk about it. Your purpose will not be to criticize the person who has left, but it will be to give group members an opportunity to process their feelings. The group members may feel a sense of rejection. Let them discuss their feelings.

You may want to have a one-to-one talk with the person who has left the group. Be reluctant to attempt talking the person into coming back. Attempt to affirm that this person is still a person of worth in your eyes and that you still want to have a good relationship. Try to leave an open door so that this individual may participate in another support group in the future.

2. What If a Spouse Does Not Understand?
What if a spouse does not understand a group member's involvement in the Heart-to-Heart group? What if a group member's spouse desperately needs recovery but is not interested? What if a spouse is threatened by the changes he or she sees in the recovering spouse even if these changes are positive?

Marriages often are built on dysfunctional rules which form a predictable but dysfunctional system. The spouse may be perplexed at the changes he or she sees. The spouse may feel angry and threatened. "I liked you better before you started going to your group," is a comment a group member might hear from a spouse.

Where emotional distance exists in family relationships, a family member may fear that this person is getting close to someone else. The dysfunctional rule is, "I do not want to get emotionally close to you, but I do not want anyone else to be emotionally close to you either."

You can help group members who experience this situation.

1. Help the group member to understand what is going on with his or her spouse. Here's a summary of what probably is happening:
   a. The rule of silence about family issues has been broken.
   b. The dysfunctional family system has been challenged.
   c. The group member may have stopped enabling the spouse to stay in some compulsive behavior.
   d. The group member has become more aware of his or her own needs.
   e. The spouse is confused and threatened by these changes.
   f. The spouse silently may be asking:
      (1) What does all this mean?
      (2) Am I losing you?
      (3) What was wrong with the way things were?
      (4) What's going on?
2. Encourage the group member's commitment to building a better marriage.
3. Encourage the group member to keep doing his or her own recovery work.
4. Remind the group member how long it took him or her to begin this healing process.
5. Affirm the group member's need to take care of himself or herself.
6. Encourage the group member never to use recovery language to manipulate or condemn the spouse.
7. Remind the group member that he or she cannot change the other person.
8. Encourage the group member to pray for the spouse.
9. Encourage the group member that spouses sometimes become open to positive change when they see real changes in a family member, but it takes time.
10. Encourage the group member to keep living by these principles even if other family members do not.

A Letter to Spouses of Group Members
The following is a letter you might choose to send to the spouses of the members of your group. Ask each group member's permission before sending the letter.

Dear (Name),
Your spouse has enrolled in a support group. During the weeks ahead your spouse will engage in a look within himself or herself that may lead to some observable changes in behavior. Your spouse may:
• Seem very introspective at times.
• Feel sad without knowing exactly why.
• Not want to do things he/she would normally want to do.

Please be patient with your spouse during this time. Spouses of people who participate in groups sometimes feel uncomfortable or even afraid of changes they see in loved ones who participate in support groups. Here are some things you can do to help your spouse and your relationship during this time.

- Be patient.
- Don't ask too many probing questions.
- Respect the confidentiality of the group.
- Give your spouse permission to deal with problem areas in the past and present.
- Try not to be threatened if your spouse wants to discuss certain aspects of your relationship. Be willing to listen and to talk.
- Understand that emotional healing takes time.
- Be willing to make positive changes in your relationship as your spouse experiences healing and growth.

If you have concerns about your spouse's involvement in the support group, discuss the matter directly and calmly with your spouse. If I can answer any questions you have, feel free to call me.

Sincerely,

Your Name

You could adapt this letter for adult children, parents, or close friends of group members who might have some questions about the group member's involvement with the group.

3. What If the Group Does Not Help Someone?
Some group members will experience more growth than others will. Most people who complete your group will indicate that the group has helped them. Occasionally, someone may not show much improvement. How will you deal with this situation?

First, realize that no one is perfect except God Himself. Your group is not perfect. Not everyone will receive the same benefits from the group. One reason for this is that some people will work more diligently on growing than will others.
Second, recognize that some people need referral to a professional counselor. They need more help than your group can give. Be willing to encourage a person to get professional help when he or she needs it, and be prepared with a list of qualified helpers from which the person may choose. Do not recommend only one specific counselor or therapist.

Apply yourself to being a good facilitator. Be open to constructive suggestions for improving your leadership. Do not berate yourself if the group does not help certain people.

Also be aware of the seed-planting aspect of your work. You may be pleasantly surprised when a group member who seemed to gain the least from the group one day approaches you and says, "You'll never know how much I have benefited from the support-group experience." Some people process information more slowly than others do; sometimes a life experience can cause a person suddenly to connect with material he or she studied months or years earlier.

Steps Toward Starting a Group

Step 1: Orient Yourself to Course Content

Read through this book and the member's book, *Moving Beyond Your Past*. Be certain you understand the goals for the group. Reading through the materials will give you an idea of what will happen during the meetings. Make sure you understand the moral inventory that begins on page 205. Review the diagrams which illustrate the cycles of recovery concept, pages 224 and the inside back cover.

Step 2: Determine Whether You Are Ready to Lead a Heart-to-Heart Support Group

In evaluating your potential as a facilitator, review the basic qualities for a Heart-to-Heart group facilitator. A qualified Heart-to-Heart group facilitator:

1. Has completed a Face-to-Face group (or other intensive family-of-origin work) and has made positive changes in his life as a result of what he has learned.
2. Has made significant progress in understanding how his past has affected his present.
3. Has developed basic skills in experiencing and expressing her own emotions.
4. Has made significant progress in overcoming compulsive behaviors resulting from childhood issues.
5. Understands that emotional health and spiritual maturity are closely related.
6. Believes that spiritual growth is a long-term process and understands that people need time to grow.
7. Is continuing to grow emotionally and spiritually.
8. Has a growing relationship with Jesus Christ that guides her attitudes and values.
9. Has a good foundation of scriptural knowledge and is an active member of a local church.
10. Receives insight and support from other people.
11. Understands the danger of trying to fix people as opposed to letting them work through their own growth process with the help of God and others.
12. Knows how to lead a group without controlling it including letting group members experience and express their feelings.
13. Is willing to give time and energy to help members of the group.

The best preparation for leading a Heart-to-Heart group is serving as an apprentice in a group led by a skilled support-group facilitator. If you do not have the opportunity to train in an apprentice relationship with a qualified group facilitator in your local church, here are some things you can do to prepare for leading a Heart-to-Heart group:

1. Participate as a member or an apprentice in a support Group Series group in another church.
2. Attend an intensive training event where qualified leaders can help you see, develop, and practice support-group facilitation skills.
3. Participate in a 12-Step group in your community.

Please do not attempt to facilitate a Heart-to-Heart group without adequate preparation. Otherwise, group members could have an experience that causes more harm than good. A bad group experience could abort your church's support-group ministry because your church could fear getting involved in the process again. We do not intend for this warning to scare you away from facilitating a support group. We intend for it to keep unprepared facilitators from getting into crises for which they are unprepared.

Step 3: Secure Approval from Church Leadership

If you are a layperson, consult the appropriate church staff member before you schedule a Heart-to-Heart support group in your church. Provide the staff member with a copy of this facilitator's guide as well as the member's book, *Moving Beyond Your Past*. Make sure the staff member understands what will occur in the group. Explain the group's goals, content, and procedures. Attempt to answer any questions the staff member may have. Give the staff member time to review the materials before you ask for approval to go ahead with the course. If you are unsure about whether you are qualified to be a support-group facilitator, ask he church staff person for guidance and be willing to hear it. If you are a church staff member, consider reviewing with appropriate lay leaders the aims of the course before you proceed. Be certain that lay leaders understand that the course is a Bible-based approach to dealing with compulsive behaviors and emotional problems.

Step 4: Order Materials

Order sufficient copies of the following materials well in advance of your first meeting: Member's book, one copy for each group member, and a copy of this facilitator's guide for your apprentice. Books may be ordered on Amazon.com. It is suggested that each group member pay for his or her own book.

Step 5: Fees

Each group member should pay for his or her own book. This helps communicate the level of commitment that is expected of group members. However, to protect your church from legal liability, do not charge fees for the group itself or pay the facilitator for group leadership. This is a lay-led group, not a professional-led group.

Step 6: Begin Skill Building

Read through the section "Actions Basic to Effective Group Leadership" in this book.

Step 7: Enlist an Apprentice

Pray about finding someone who will go through the group as a participant but who also displays a willingness to lead a group later. Consider individuals who have participated or led in other support groups in your church. Look for people who have made significant progress in dealing with compulsive behaviors in their lives.

You may choose this person from individuals who sign up for the group, or you may want to enlist someone who appears to have the appropriate skills for facilitating a group, even though he or she did not sign up for the study. Training the proper apprentice is very important.

Step 8: Set a Date and Time for Starting the Group

Schedule 13 meetings of the group. Ideally, the schedule should be as free as possible from interruptions such as holidays. We suggest a registration period of at least three weeks. Stop registration one week before the first meeting since we ask group members to complete five daily assignments before the first session.

If you decide to offer the Heart-to-Heart groups year round, a good schedule is to have one group starting in early fall, one group starting in January, and another group starting in late spring or early summer. This provides enough time between each set of groups to register and to prepare for the next group. It also gives group facilitators a needed break.

Set a starting time that will be convenient for group members. Allow at least two hours for each session.

Step 9: Find a Place to Meet

Conduct the group in the same place each week. The room where the group meets should be quiet and private enough so group members feel free to talk and express emotions. Avoid a location and schedule which would result in children running through a nearby hallway or peeking through the door.

Make sure the person on your church staff who assigns rooms for meetings does not schedule meetings in rooms directly adjacent to the place where the group meets. An atmosphere in which noise and distractions occur will make group members anxious and unwilling to share. The best meeting place usually will be in the church building at a time when few other activities are in progress. Meeting in a person's home is not recommended.

A room with an entrance away from the main entrance to the church building is helpful. Group members need to be able to come and go without worrying that others will ask them where they have been or what they are doing. Some group members may cry during a meeting. Members of the group need to be able to leave the meeting without worrying about being seen after they have obviously been crying. Scheduling a group meeting during the hours just before a church's worship service is not ideal since group members often need undistracted time just after the meeting to process what has occurred and new insights gained.

The meeting room should be large enough to hold a circle of about eight chairs without the members feeling cramped. The room should be clean and comfortable. Windows are OK unless they are placed in such a way that passersby can look inside and make group members feel uncomfortable. Be sure that restrooms are accessible to the meeting room.

Step 10: Decide on Child Care

Decide whether you will provide child care for group members' children. The advantage of offering child care is that it may enable some people to attend who could not participate otherwise. The disadvantage is that support-group meetings sometimes run late. You need the freedom to let the meeting last a little longer if a group member is doing some significant sharing. Child care could become a handicap if group members feel the need to leave the meeting early so they can take children home. The best solution usually is for group members to secure child care on their own. A group member's spouse can offer encouragement by keeping the couple's children as a gift to the member.

Step 11: Advertise the Group

How can you let others know about your group? First, decide on your target audience. I recommend that you target people who have completed a Face-to-Face group or some similar support group which focuses on dealing with childhood issues. Communicate with all people who have completed Face-to-Face groups. Consider advertising outside your church to reach people who have done the necessary foundational work for participating in a Heart-to-Heart group.

This group is an alternative to a 12-Step group. If you are not familiar with the 12 Steps, they form the foundation for various recovery groups like Alcoholics Anonymous. Our Christ-centered study offers another way of working through the issues the 12 Steps address. This approach will attract some people in your community who have attended secular recovery groups and are looking for a Christian recovery group. Often, you will find that these people have received help from the groups they have attended, yet they hunger for a group such as this one in which they freely can integrate their Christian faith with the principles of recovery.

Announce in your church the fact that the group is forming. Use the church newsletter to advertise the group. Once you complete your first group, you will find that word-of-mouth comments are your strongest publicity. A successful group will lead to new people asking you for information about the next group.

Be sure to have a phone number available where interested people always can get specific information about when the next group will be offered. Designate one specific person who will receive all inquiries about the group. This ensures that callers receive accurate information and helps build trust. People frequently share confidential issues during the initial inquiry about the group.

Once a group starts, other people may express an interest. The Heart-to-Heart group is a closed group. Add no one to the group after the first meeting. If you list the meeting time of your group in your church bulletin, indicate that this group is closed, but announce a date when a second group will begin. This will prevent interested individuals from showing up at your meeting only to learn that the group is closed. If you have adequate leadership, begin registration for your second group as soon as you have one person who is ready to commit to a second group. You may find you have a full group signed up before the first group has finished the study.

Step 12: Interview Prospective Group Members

The group will work best if you have at least three group members besides yourself. The group should contain no more than eight people including yourself. If the group fills up, record additional names, and start another group when you have enough members and a qualified facilitator.

Meet personally with each person who expresses an interest in being a member of the group. During this time, show the person a copy of the book *Moving Beyond Your Past* and cover the following points.

• Discuss the Goals of the Group

Discuss the group's goals listed in the introduction of the member's book. Talk about the group's purpose. Ask whether participants have any questions about the purpose.

• Explain that Spouses Should Be in Separate Groups

If a person's spouse is interested in participating, explain that he or she will need to be in a separate group. See concept 9 on page 13.

• Explain the Covenant

Review the covenant that follows the introduction in the member's book. Explain that one must be willing to sign the covenant to participate in the group. Ask whether the individual has any questions about the covenant. Ask the individual to sign the covenant in your presence. Keep a signed copy on file.

• Explain Daily Assignments

Review the daily assignments for unit 1 in the member's book. Explain that participating in the group requires a willingness to spend 30 to 60 minutes a day five days a week working on the assignments. Ask the prospective group member to complete the assignments in daily segments rather than back-to-back in one day. Many of the assignments are reflective in nature. Like vitamins, they don't work properly if you consume five days' worth in one day. Explain that participants should complete the assignments for unit 1 before they attend the first session.

• Discuss a Commitment

The individual may commit immediately to participating in the group. If so, ask the individual to purchase the member's book and sign the covenant in his or her book. Keep a copy of the signed covenant for your records. Record the person's name, address, phone number, and church affiliation. Write down the date, day, time, and place of the first session and give it to the registrant.

Remind the new group member that any person who misses more than three sessions may be asked to drop out of the group. The members of the group will make this decision. Also, emphasize that attendance at the first meeting of the group is mandatory. If the group member cannot attend the first meeting, she can wait and participate in the group when the church offers it again.

The individual may want to think about committing to the group. If she wants to think about her decision to participate in the group, encourage her to do so. Let her know how to contact you when she makes the decision. If the group is nearly full (We recommend a maximum size of eight people including yourself.) let this person know that others may register and that the group soon may be full. Inform this person of the final deadline for group registration (usually one week before the first session).

Be sensitive to determining whether a financial problem is making it impossible for the prospective member to purchase the materials for the group. When possible, offer help. Avoid turning anyone away because of a lack of money. A scholarship fund helps in providing help in such cases.

• Reassure the Prospective Group Member

Explain that at no time will any group member be forced to do or say anything against his will. Group members will be challenged lovingly to confront their compulsive behaviors but always will have freedom of choice about what they do.

If you can do so sincerely, offer to pray for this person as he prepares for the first meeting. Make yourself available to answer any further questions.

Step 13: Prepare a Group Roster and Name Tags

When you have completed the registration process, make a roster including all group members to use as an attendance roll for the group meetings.

Prepare an attractive, reusable name tag for each group member. Include first and last names. Heart-to-Heart groups are confidential but not anonymous. Plan to distribute the name tags at the beginning of each session and to take them up at the end of each session.

Step 14: Pray for Each Group Member

Begin praying regularly for each group member. Pray especially that God will remove any fears each person may have about being in this group. Pray that God will help you lead the group effectively.

Step 15: Begin the Sessions

Review the session guides for each of the 13 meetings to get a sense of how the meetings will unfold. Carefully review the session guide for session one. Call the registered group members before the first meeting to make sure they are clear on time and place.

Your call also will encourage them to follow through and attend the first meeting.

Step 16: Help Group Members Plan for Follow-Up

About halfway through the study begin talking to members of your group about follow-up options. Refer to pages 203-204 in the member's book for a list of ways members can continue in their spiritual growth.

Some group members may decide to seek one-to-one counseling with a professional counselor. Help these group members by referring them to competent Christian counselors. When you make a referral, always offer the person a choice of at least two or three counselors. Do not assume the responsibility of choosing the person's counselor for him or her. By suggesting a choice of counselors, you also can avoid legal liability.

Other group members may be ready to do some work on their own. Help them to develop a specific plan for continuing the recovery process.

Overview of Heart-to-Heart Group Sessions

The following group-session plans will help you facilitate meaningful sharing times for your Heart-to-Heart Support Group. Here is an overview of what you will find on the following pages:

Session Goal. The goal describes an anticipated outcome of the session. Keep in mind that members will progress at their own unique pace. Do not get discouraged if you do not achieve these goals each week. The group members are your ministry. Be sensitive to their needs. Allow the Lord to guide you in meeting those needs. What He wants to do in their lives may surpass any goal you may set for the session. Pray regularly that God will be your constant Guide throughout this process.

What to Expect. Based on my experience as a support-group facilitator, I have provided you with insights about what may happen during your sessions for each week. Based on the content the members study, new experiences will confront you week after week. These paragraphs are designed to alert you to potential experiences that may arise during the session.

Skill Development. I have made the assumption that you already know the activities basic to effective group leadership. We design these sessions each week as continuing education for you. Take time to review the activities necessary to effective group leadership on the page number listed. Then observe my suggestions for developing or fine-tuning your skill during the session.

Before the Session. If you will read through this list carefully and will complete each of the actions, you should be ready for the group session. Place a check mark beside each item as you complete it. Most of these actions are repeated from week to week, so they will become routine by the end of the 13 weeks.

Each week the sessions will encourage you to review the self-evaluation checklist on page 29. Be sure to take time before each session mentally to walk through the list.

During the Session. A standard Heart-to-Heart group session includes discussion questions and a closing circle of prayer, which we describe in **Closing the Session.** Throughout the session, watch for times that the Lord may impress you to stop and to allow the group to pray for a member. God will work through the members of the group to comfort, challenge, or encourage a needy member. This is a practical way to keep your group Christ-centered.

After the Session. We provide this checklist to help you evaluate the session and to begin preparing for the following session. Check each of the items as you complete it. I encourage you not to skip the process of keeping a journal. It will prove to be a valuable vehicle for skill building and will assist your memory about members' needs and about their progress as you pray for those in your group.

May the Lord work through you in a wonderful way to bring His healing to the painful memories of your group members and to help them apply their knowledge to their present relationships and circumstances. Give God the credit and the glory for all that occurs in your group.

Facilitator's Self-Evaluation Checklist

Use this handy checklist after each meeting to evaluate your role as a facilitator of that meeting. After you have evaluated your progress as a facilitator in each of the areas listed below, put a check in the box for that session.

	Sessions												
	1	2	3	4	5	6	7	8	9	10	11	12	13
Am I willing to let the needs of the group members guide the agenda of the meeting?	❏	❏	❏	❏	❏	❏	❏	❏	❏	❏	❏	❏	❏
Do I feel that I must solve every problem?	❏	❏	❏	❏	❏	❏	❏	❏	❏	❏	❏	❏	❏
Am I afraid of anger or conflict?	❏	❏	❏	❏	❏	❏	❏	❏	❏	❏	❏	❏	❏
Do I feel a need to give easy answers?	❏	❏	❏	❏	❏	❏	❏	❏	❏	❏	❏	❏	❏
Can I accept periods of silence in a group meeting?	❏	❏	❏	❏	❏	❏	❏	❏	❏	❏	❏	❏	❏
Am I willing to let group members cry?	❏	❏	❏	❏	❏	❏	❏	❏	❏	❏	❏	❏	❏
Am I willing to lovingly confront group members when necessary?	❏	❏	❏	❏	❏	❏	❏	❏	❏	❏	❏	❏	❏
Can I accept group members as they are?	❏	❏	❏	❏	❏	❏	❏	❏	❏	❏	❏	❏	❏
Am I willing to do what I ask group members to do?	❏	❏	❏	❏	❏	❏	❏	❏	❏	❏	❏	❏	❏
Am I willing to feel my own emotions?	❏	❏	❏	❏	❏	❏	❏	❏	❏	❏	❏	❏	❏
Am I willing to share my own emotional pain with others in my life?	❏	❏	❏	❏	❏	❏	❏	❏	❏	❏	❏	❏	❏
Am I willing to be honest with my group?	❏	❏	❏	❏	❏	❏	❏	❏	❏	❏	❏	❏	❏
Am I ready to be emotionally present with my group?	❏	❏	❏	❏	❏	❏	❏	❏	❏	❏	❏	❏	❏

RECOVERY

♦ **Session Goal**

Each group member will introduce himself or herself to the group and will share something about the problems that are prompting him or her to participate in the group.

What to Expect

The first meeting of your group sets the tone for all future meetings. This meeting is the time for bonding. If you have some group members who were all in one Face-to-Face group together previously along with others who were not part of that group, this meeting is especially crucial for bringing all people present into a sense of being one new group. During this meeting you can help group members understand how the focus of this group differs from that of a Face-to-Face group.

Skill Development

Before this first meeting, take some time to reread the entire section on "Actions Basic to Effective Group Leadership," page 16. Give special attention to developing skills at these activities this week:

❑ **1. Be personally involved without relinquishing leadership (page 16).** Your attitude and involvement during the first meeting will set the tone for how each member of the group shares in this and future meetings. During this meeting you will ask each group member to respond to several questions, including his or her answers to a series of questions found at the end of unit 1, day 5. You will begin by sharing your responses to these questions first. Your level of honesty and emotional involvement will set the example for the other group members. As you share, you may become emotional. Don't worry about that. You are modeling what you want your group members to do. Do not act out a level of emotional response you do not feel. Be yourself, but be willing to share something that hurts.

❑ **2. Communicate acceptance and concern (page 16).** During the meeting group members will share painful matters. Some of them will talk openly about things they seldom or never talk about. They will feel afraid and vulnerable. Your attitude and actions can create an atmosphere of acceptance and concern. When a group member is sharing and has to stop because he is crying, say, "I support you. It is OK to cry. This is a safe place to talk about this." Some group members will feel much shame about the things they are talking about. Some may feel ashamed of even being present in the group. Be open to ways to communicate to each person an attitude of love and acceptance.

❑ **3. Create a feeling of safety in the group (page 17).** Remind the group that all that takes place in the group meetings is confidential. Affirm your commitment to maintaining confidentiality. If you have a counselor who is supervising you or a support-group ministry team with whom you consult, mention that you sometimes will need to confer with that person or group on issues arising out of the group meetings. Affirm that your supervisor or group also is committed to confidentiality.

Communicate confidence in the way you lead the group. You can be open about your own emotional pain while you still show that you are confident about your leadership.

When the meeting starts, make sure all doors to the room are closed. You may need to put some "Meeting in Progress" signs on doors to keep people from interrupting. Explain to the group members that they do not have to be Christians to participate in the group but that the group will include references to Christ's power to help with our emotional problems. Unchurched group members may fear that you somehow will pressure them toward your beliefs. Your comments at this time can allay such fears. Unbelieving group members often are won to Christ when they experience the nonmanipulative love of the support group throughout a period of weeks.

❑ **4. Keep the group operating on a feeling level (page 18).** If all your Heart-to-Heart group ever does is have intellectual discussions on compulsive behavior issues, you will not give much help to anyone. One of the goals of the group is "to help group members become more sensitive to their own feelings." This meeting is a model for all the other meetings. The group needs to operate on a feeling level in this meeting. Usually, this happens naturally as people talk about heartfelt struggles. You are the key person. You will set the tone by how you share your own story.

Before the Meeting

❏ Pray for yourself and the group members.
❏ Re-check the church calendar to be certain no one else is scheduled to use the room where you will be meeting.
❏ If you are providing child care, make sure the child-care workers are prepared to stay as late as necessary. The first meeting often runs longer than other meetings do.
❏ Place directional signs at all outside church entrances that lead to your meeting room.
❏ Check to be sure air conditioning or heating is set properly.
❏ Be sure the room is clean. Arrange in a circle the exact number of chairs needed.
❏ Have several boxes of tissue ready.
❏ Have a legal pad and pen ready to take notes.
❏ Be sure you have a name tag ready for each group member.
❏ Review the Facilitator's Self-Evaluation Checklist on page 29.

During the Meeting

1. Greet the group members as they arrive for the meeting. Give out name tags.
2. Give each person his or her name tag.
3. Start the meeting at the scheduled time.
4. Use the following question as a springboard to start discussion: How did participation in a Face-to-Face group affect your life? Begin by sharing your answer to this question.
5. Lead the group through the outline of the Cycle of Pain (inside back cover in the member's book) that characterizes adult children of dysfunctional families.
6. Use a chalkboard or marker board if available. On it write the following statements:
   • Your childhood family is out of control, and you feel deep emotional pain.
   • You develop a survival system which utilizes some form of compulsive behavior to ease the pain.
   • You deny the existence and the negative impact of your compulsive behavior.

• You may manage to keep your denial system in place, or your denial system may break down.
• You experience brokenness.
• You make a decision:
   Try to rebuild compulsion/denial system, or
   Acknowledge brokenness and surrender to God.
• You experience further pain or begin the recovery process depending on the decision you made.
   Ask group members to discuss this cycle. Can they identify with it? Where do they feel they are now in this cycle?
7. Lead the group members in discussing the following questions:

┌───┐
│ • Do you have a denial system?   │
│ • What is it?   │
│ • How does it work?   │
│ • What compulsive behaviors do you plan to │
│   work on in this group?   │
│ • Where are you in regard to Turning Point 1? │
└───┘

8. Share three of the five statements you wrote on page 28 in the member's book which describe what your life would be like in a state of spiritual and emotional health. Share your answers to the questions first. Answer the fourth question in terms of something you are working on personally, not in terms of your role as leader. After you have shared, call on someone else to share. Don't go around the circle. Ask someone to volunteer, or choose the person who seems most ready to be the next one to share.

While the other group members share, take notes on a legal pad. You will not take notes during any of the other meetings. You need to make notes during this meeting because what the group members share in this meeting becomes the foundation for the rest of the work they do. Your notes will help you remember the key details of each person's story. Do not stop anyone who is sharing because you are behind on your notes. Just write down what you can. Work diligently to look at the person who is talking even though you are taking notes. Don't give up on being a good listener while you are taking notes. Before you begin sharing, explain to the group members that you will take notes while they speak. Tell them that this is a privilege reserved for the group facilitator. Ask them to have nothing in their hands or laps during the meeting. This includes their *Moving Beyond Your Past* books.

Estimate how much time you have for each person to share. Don't rush anyone, but if a group member gets way off target on time, step in to encourage and redirect toward a conclusion. End the meeting after everyone has shared.

Closing the Meeting

1. Commend the group members for their sharing. If you have time, ask group members to share what they are feeling about the first session.
2. Remind the group members to complete each of the five daily assignments before the next meeting.
3. Close the meeting with a circle of prayer. Ask group members to stand and join hands. Encourage group members to pray for the strength to make the five statements they wrote about a recovery lifestyle a reality. Ask group members to pray for each other. If a group members does not feel comfortable praying aloud, ask him simply to say amen when his time to pray arrives.

After the Meeting

❑ Collect the name tags.
❑ Mark attendance on the group roster.
❑ Look over the notes you took during the meeting. Keep the notes for later review.
❑ If someone signed up for the group but did not attend the first meeting, contact that person. Because so much group bonding takes place during the first meeting, anyone who missed the first meeting should wait for the group to be offered again.
❑ Evaluate your skill-building work.

• Was I personally and emotionally involved in the meeting while still leading the meeting?
• What are some things I did or said to communicate acceptance and concern?
• What did I do to create a feeling of safety within the group?
• Did I help the group members stay emotionally involved in what was happening?

Consider keeping a journal during the time you lead the group. Start now by making an entry indicating how you feel about leading the group. What emotions did you feel as you led the first meeting? What questions do you have that are unanswered?

Group Session 2	BROKENNESS

◆ Session Goal

Group members will identify areas of brokenness in their lives.

What to Expect

Group members are still "checking out" the group. They may feel fearful of talking about their compulsive behaviors with the group. Some still are not sure how this group process is going to work. It doesn't feel quite like a Face-to-Face group. Be sensitive to the need that many adult children from dysfunctional families feel that they must know what will happen next. Let group members know where you are heading with the group.

Skill Development

Work on developing skills at these activities this week:

❑ **1. Teach group members how to help each other (page 12).** Last week group members focused on sharing their own issues. This week you will have more time to help group members work on helping each other. Remind the group members about the following guidelines:

• When a group member is struggling, say, "I support you." Group members may say this at any time. They do not need a cue from the facilitator. After a group member has shared, be willing to give feedback. What were you as the facilitator feeling when the group member was sharing? What you were feeling may help the group member know what he was feeling. If the facilitator does not ask a group member to give feedback, a group member can say, "May I give some feedback?" With the permission of the facilitator and the person to whom the member is offering the feedback, the group member may proceed.

• Think about how you phrase your statements. "I feel that you are experiencing a lot of fear about letting go of this compulsive behavior," is better than "You're obviously afraid of this group."

• If the person sitting next to you is struggling, express concern. For example, you might gently place your hand on this person's shoulder. It is OK for a group member to say to someone who is struggling, "May I give you a hug?" Be sure you have given the person enough time to finish expressing his feelings before you offer a hug. Do not use hugs to help a person get away from his feelings.

• Remind the group that you as facilitator will guide, not control, the meeting. Group members take their cues from you. At the same time, they can take the initiative to offer help to one another.

❑ **2. Facilitate feedback (page 17).** Feedback is an emotional mirror within the group which helps group members get in touch with their feelings. Feedback also helps group members see themselves more objectively. Feedback can help group members be more honest with themselves about their own compulsive behaviors.

Feedback occurs when I tell you what I see and hear you saying. You may not be aware of the messages your facial expressions, body language, and even your words communicate. What is obvious to me as I watch and listen may be unknown to you, but I can help you see what I see by giving you feedback.

Feedback is nonjudgmental. When I give feedback, I am not insisting that what I say is the way things are. I am simply reporting what I see and hear. Through feedback group members begin to discover what reality is. At some point shutting out reality became a way of coping. A selective screening of reality became habitual. Feedback brings us back in touch with reality.

Hopefully, members of your group already have some feedback skills. You set the example, then give them some room to follow it. After you have explained and modeled the concept, consciously wait long enough for other group members to give feedback. Let them learn that you will not always be the first one to speak. Watch the faces of group members as they listen to someone else share. If you see strong emotion in facial expressions or other body language, ask that person if she is willing to give some feedback.

❏ **3. Help group members identify what they are feeling (page 18).** Identifying emotions is important in this study because people often use compulsive behaviors to mask emotional pain. Help group members to get in touch with their feelings during the meetings.

When you observe intense emotions in a particular group member you might ask, "Do you ever engage in compulsive behavior to deal with this emotion?" During the Face-to-Face group, group members were asked to focus on a narrow range of feelings: anger, fear, guilt, joy, loneliness, sadness, and shame. In this group you are placing more emphasis on changing present behaviors and less emphasis on identifying feelings. However, helping group members identify what they are feeling as the meeting unfolds still is important.

Group members may now begin to identify a wider range of feelings. Sometimes when you ask a group member, "What are you feeling?" you will get an answer like, "I am feeling compassion." This calls for some probing. If the person making this statement is codependent, the sense of feeling compassion may be legitimate or it may be a cover for feeling one's own feelings. Codependent individuals transfer their personal emotions over to others. Help each member identify his own feelings.

2. Start the meeting on time.

3. Lead the group in discussing the following questions:

- Do you have a denial system? What is it? How does it work?
- Has your denial system broken yet? If yes, how did it break? If no, what will it take to break it?
- Discuss some ways denial systems break.
  a. You get tired.
  b. You get scared.
  c. You get caught.
  d. You lose team support.
- Name one or two compulsive behaviors you plan to work on in this group.
- What kinds of brokenness do you bring to this group?
  a. Possibilities
  b. Broken promises (given or received)
  c. Broken heart
  d. Broken relationships
  e. Broken spirit
  f. Broken will
  g. Broken boundaries
  h. Other

Before the Meeting

❏ Pray for yourself and the group members.
❏ If possible, call each group member to let him/her know you are looking forward to seeing him/her at the second meeting.
❏ Review the notes you took on each group member during the last meeting.
❏ Check to be sure air conditioning or heating is set properly.
❏ Be sure the room is clean with the exact number of chairs needed arranged in a circle.
❏ Have several boxes of tissue ready.
❏ Review the Facilitator's Self-Evaluation Checklist on page 29.

During the Meeting

1. Greet the group members as they arrive. Give out name tags.

Closing the Meeting

1. Remind the group members to complete each of the five daily assignments before they attend the next meeting.
2. Close the meeting with a circle of prayer. Invite group members to hold hands as they sit in a circle. Encourage each group member to pray about something that he or she is feeling now or something that happened in this meeting.

After the Meeting

❏ Collect the name tags.
❏ Mark attendance on the group roster.
❏ If you are keeping a journal, record your thoughts and feelings about the meeting.
❏ Evaluate your skill-building work.
- What did I do during this meeting to teach group members to help one another in the group process?

- What evidences did I see to indicate that group members were learning to help one another in the group process?
- What did I do to facilitate feedback in the group?
- Did I help group members learn to give feedback to one another?

SURRENDER

> ### ♦ Session Goal
>
> You will challenge group members to make a full surrender of their lives to God.

What to Expect

Some group members will know immediately that surrender is an issue for them. Others may respond with, "I already have surrendered my life to God. I am a Christian. The need to surrender does not apply to me." You will need to help the latter group understand that when we engage in excessive control of our lives, surrender is an issue. The challenge to surrender raises trust issues. Group members may need to talk about problems they have in trusting other people and in trusting God.

Skill Development

Work on developing skills at these activities this week:

❑ **1. Be willing to confront in love (page 16).** Remember that you cannot effectively lead this group if you are unwilling to confront. If you habitually avoid conflict, you will not be effective as the leader of the group.

Watch for signs of denial. A group member says he does not have a problem with surrender. In each of the previous meetings this group member may have shown a continuing need to be in control.

You wait for the right opportunity. You say, "Jim, you are telling us that you do not have a problem with surrender, but you are communicating a strong need to be in control." Ideally the group member then would respond. He may continue in denial. If he does, ask him, "Would you be willing to get some feedback from other members of the group?" With his permission, call on other group members to comment on their observations about surrender in his life. If two or three

members agree with you, ask him to respond again. Hopefully he will start to listen. When he does, you can begin to explore effectively the depth and the sources of his unwillingness to surrender.

Confrontation motivated by love is sensitive to timing and wording. It is not hostile or destructive. It is sensitive to how much the recipient can deal with at the time of the confrontation.

❑ **2. Help group members identify what they are feeling (page 18).** Identifying emotions is important in this study because people often use compulsive behaviors to mask emotional pain. During the meetings help group members to get in touch with their feelings. When you observe intense emotions in a particular group member, you might ask, "Do you ever engage in compulsive behavior to deal with this emotion?"

When a group member obviously is detached while others in the group are very emotionally involved, you can ask, "What are you feeling?" The person may seem perplexed at her inability to name a feeling. She has shut down emotionally. This may feel so normal for her that she does not realize she is out of sync with the emotional tone of the people around her.

Ask, "Do you think it is unusual that while everyone else in the group is involved deeply at an emotional level, you are not?" Through this process, you may help a group member identify the fact that she has shut down some basic emotional responses.

A key element in keeping the group on a feeling level is your willingness to stay in touch with your own feelings. If you refuse to allow yourself to feel your emotions, the group will follow your lead. Do not be afraid to say at various points in the meeting, "I am feeling some sadness," or "I am feeling some pain right now."

❑ **3. Help group members connect the past with the present (page 18).** Help group members connect present difficulties with surrender to past relationships with authority figures. Help them to question themselves to learn the origins of their trust issues.

Before the Meeting

❑ Pray for yourself and the group members.
❑ Review the notes you took on each group member during the first meeting.
❑ Check to be sure air conditioning or heating is set properly.
❑ Be sure the room is clean with the exact number of chairs needed arranged in a circle.
❑ Have several boxes of tissue ready.
❑ Review the Facilitator's Self-Evaluation Checklist on page 29.

During the Meeting

1. Greet the group members as they arrive. Give out name tags.
2. Use the following discussion questions as a springboard for getting the group interaction started.

- How do you relate to authority figures? Do you give mixed messages to authority figures? Why do you relate to authority figures the way you do?
- Read Galatians 5:22-23. Remind the group members that the fruit of the spirit also are attributes of God. Then ask this question: Do you need to rework your heartfelt view of God? Why? Is it out of line with what the Bible says about God?
- What is one broken area of your life that needs to be surrendered to God?
- How do you feel about surrendering this part of your life to God?
- How are you doing with the compulsive behavior(s) you have chosen to work on during this group?

Closing the Meeting

During this meeting you will talk to group members about beginning work on the moral inventory. The moral inventory is a separate section of the book. See pages 205-219 of the member's book. Group members will have four weeks to complete the inventory. Daily readings for the next four weeks will lead group members through the inventory.

Group members may be intimidated by the scope of the inventory. Warn them of the danger of perfectionism/procrastination. They may find themselves saying, "I don't feel like doing this perfectly now, so I will do it later." Encourage group members to complete a little work each day.

Close the meeting with the circle of prayer. Ask group members to stand and join hands. Invite each group member to say a sentence prayer for the person on his or her right, asking God to help this person to surrender any area of his life that he or she is holding back.

After the Meeting

❑ Collect the name tags.
❑ Mark attendance on the group roster.
❑ If you are keeping a journal, record your thoughts and feelings about the meeting.
❑ Ask yourself these questions:
  - Can you remember a time during this week's meeting that you confronted a group member? If the answer is "Yes," how did you communicate love and acceptance while you confronted?
  - What did you do during this meeting to help group members identify their emotions?
  - Group members need to connect past experiences and their present problems with surrender. How did you help them do this?

CLEANSING

♦ **Session Goal**

Group members will share their reactions to beginning work on the moral inventory.

What to Expect

Group members have started working on their moral inventories. Alert group members to several common reactions that people have when they begin work on the moral inventory.
- This is overwhelming. I can't do it.
- When I do this, I want to do it perfectly. I must do it later.
- I never will be able to share this information with another person.
- I am overwhelmed by the deficiencies in my life.

Encourage group members to refuse to be overwhelmed by the task of completing the moral inventory. Challenge them to avoid the temptation of writing "perfect" answers to the questions on the inventory. Lead them to focus on writing the answers as opposed to worrying about how they will be able to talk about the answers with another person. Encourage them to share with the group any feelings of inadequacy that may result from working on the inventory.

Remind members that they may need to use additional sheets of paper as they work on their moral inventories.

Skill Development

Work on developing skill at these activities this week:

❑ **1. Help group members understand psychological expression of biblical truth (page 18).** Remind group members of God's grace. Remind them of the words of Romans 5:8: "While we were yet sinners, Christ died for us." Help group members accept the grace of God at an experiential level. Help them to sense God's love even as they confront the weaknesses and failures of their lives. Help them to feel God's love and acceptance through the love and acceptance the group displays. Take the lead by modeling caring acceptance toward each group member.

❑ **2. Communicate acceptance and concern (page 16).** Developing this skill is particularly important at this stage because working on the moral inventory may awaken new feelings of shame and guilt on the part of group members.

❑ **3. Utilize good listening skills (page 16).** Some things you may need to work on:
- When one group member is speaking, occasionally make a visual scan of the other group members. What are they saying nonverbally?
- Remember occasionally to restate and summarize what a group member has just said to the group. Then ask, "Is that what you said?" Let the group member respond.
- Remember to face the person who is speaking and to lean toward the speaker.
- When appropriate, nod your head to show you are hearing what others are saying. Use an occasional verbal phrase to indicate you are listening.
- When necessary, stop the speaker and ask for clarification of what he or she just said.
- Make sure someone in the group gives some response when a person says something that needs a response.

❑ **4. Know how to close a meeting (page 19).** Occasionally a group member may surprise you by saying something like, "I'm not going to be able to stay much longer. I'm not feeling well." Along with the words you hear, you may hear a nonverbal message, "I am not willing to stay much longer, and I think you should end the meeting." If you are getting this message from several people in the group, you may need to conclude the meeting. If the statement is originating from one person, you may be dealing with a control issue. The person may be experiencing some fear about facing the issues that you are addressing. Encourage such a person to stay present until the meeting is over. You may want to ask, "Is something about this meeting making you uncomfortable?" You may need to say, "You have my permission to leave early while we stay to finish the meeting." Do not let a controlling person manipulate your group by using such comments to determine when the meeting will end. If a group member tries to force an early end to more than one meeting, you will need to address that with the individual. A group member should not leave the group meetings early repeatedly without the matter being addressed by the facilitator and/or the group.

Remember to be flexible about the time of closing the meeting, but do not consistently end the meeting significantly later than the target time for adjourning. About 30 minutes before you are ready to close the meeting, help the person on whom you are focusing reach a point of closure. Then ask, "Does anyone else have anything you need to talk about?" Take some time to respond to issues others raise in response to your question. At some point you will need to cut off the discussion. Affirm the importance of what people are saying. Offer to pick up with the same topic next time. Ask the group member to introduce the topic at the beginning of the next meeting. This helps the group member exercise responsibility for taking care of himself rather than expecting the group leader to take care of him.

Be sure you have tied up loose ends. Did you put someone on hold during the meeting? Did you ever get back to her? Was someone interrupted in sharing as you moved to focus on another group member's response to her? Did you get closure with the original speaker?

End the meeting in the manner described under "Closing the Meeting." End with the closing prayer. After the closing prayer, the meeting is over. Do not restart the meeting after the closing prayer.

Before the Meeting

❏ Pray for yourself and the group members.
❏ Review the notes you took on each group member during the first meeting.
❏ Check to be sure air conditioning or heating is set properly.
❏ Be sure the room is clean with the exact number of chairs needed arranged in a circle.
❏ Have several boxes of tissue ready.
❏ Write the discussion questions on a poster or chalkboard and display them in the meeting room.
❏ Review the Facilitator's Self-Evaluation Checklist on page 29.

During the Meeting

1. Greet the group members as they arrive. Give out name tags.
2. Use the following discussion questions as a guide for the meeting.

> - What are some feelings you had this week as you began working on your moral inventory?
> - Has one particular aspect of the moral inventory been especially difficult for you?
> - How are you feeling about sharing your moral inventory with someone else?
> - Have you learned anything from working on your moral inventory that you would like to share with the group?
> - How are you doing with the compulsive behavior(s) you have chosen to work on during this group?

Closing the Meeting

1. Bring the group to a point of closure on the issues raised during the meeting.
2. Encourage group members to pray for each other daily. Do not do this in a shaming way. Encourage your group to be faithful in this activity.

After the Meeting

❏ Collect the name tags.
❏ Mark attendance on the group roster.
❏ If you are keeping a journal, record your thoughts and feelings on the meeting.
❏ Evaluate your skill-building work. What did you say or do in this meeting to help group members develop a better understanding of God's grace?

Place a check in the margin by the side of each listening skill trait you practiced during this meeting.
- When one group member is speaking, occasionally make a visual scan of the other group members. What are they saying nonverbally?

- Remember to occasionally restate and summarize what a group member has just said to the group. Then ask, "Is that what you said?" Let the group member respond.
- Remember to face the person who is speaking and to lean toward the speaker.
- When appropriate, nod your head to show you are hearing what is being said. Use an occasional verbal phrase to indicate you are listening.
- When necessary, stop the speaker and ask him or her to clarify what he or she just said.
- Make sure someone in the group gives some response when a person says something that needs a response.

❏ Evaluate the way in which you closed the meeting.
  - Were you sensitive to the needs of the group as you decided when to close the meeting?
  - Did you bring each issue raised to a point of closure?
  - Were you sensitive to any unmet needs as you moved toward closing the meeting?
  - Did you encourage group members to introduce unfinished topics at the next meeting?
  - Did you stop the meeting after the circle of prayer?
  - Did you permit one group member to unduly influence the time when the meeting ended?
  - What did you do to communicate acceptance and concern?

HONESTY

What to Expect

Group members may be struggling with the moral inventory. Some may approach it with a perfectionistic attitude. Others may be procrastinating. They plan to do it perfectly, but they don't feel like doing it perfectly now. Others may feel overwhelmed by the moral inventory. Use this session to encourage group members as they continue work on the moral inventory.

Group members should complete the moral inventory this week and next and share the contents with another person. Group members may need help in finding an appropriate person with whom to share.

Be prepared for the strong possibility that some group members will not finish this assignment on time. Encourage group members who do not finish the moral inventory by the seventh session to keep working on it. Some group members may not finish the moral inventory for several more weeks after that. The main thing is to encourage the group members to keep working on the inventory. You can help a group member who is having a difficult time completing this task by giving him or her opportunities to discuss what is blocking completion of the moral inventory.

Skill Development

Work on developing skill at these activities this week:

❑ **1. Validate feelings (page 20).** Even though a Heart-to-Heart group is more focused on dealing with current compulsive behaviors than it is on identifying feelings, you still can help group members stay in touch with their feelings.

When a group member identifies a feeling, be careful to let her know that feeling that emotion is OK right now and that you are glad she expressed what she was feeling. Use statements like, "I know it must have been difficult for you to share that. Thank you for exercising the courage to share."

A group member may weep convulsively, then apologize. A good response would be to ask several group members, "How do you feel about Jim's crying? Does it make you respect him less?" You will know which group members to ask for a healthy response, and you can expect them to respond with words like, "I admire someone who can let his emotions out. I support Jim for being able to cry."

Avoid telling a person that she is feeling the wrong thing or that she is wrong for having a certain feeling. Your group will contain people who have trouble even finding their feelings. Once they find a feeling, they need help in learning how to name the feeling and then in deciding how to respond to it.

❑ **2. Keep one person from dominating the group (page 19).** Since most or all of your group members have been in one or more support groups before this one, this should be less of a problem. However, you may have one person in your group who is very needy or whose personality causes him or her to dominate. Remember some of the ways in which a person may dominate a group:

- Claiming a major portion of each group meeting to talk about his issues
- Attempting to move the group toward an early dismissal if he is uncomfortable with what is happening
- Repeatedly waiting until the last 10 minutes of a meeting to introduce an emotional bombshell
- Attempting to block other group members' expressions of emotions
- Making efforts to shame you as group facilitator through repeated hostile challenges to your leadership
- Criticizing the motives or feelings of other group members
- Repeatedly trying to rescue other group members who are receiving needed confrontation

The key in determining whether a group member is dominating the group is to look for repeated behavior. A person may or may not be aware that he or she is attempting to dominate the group. That is not the point. If you permit a group member to dominate group meetings, your group's effectiveness will be destroyed.

The first step in dealing with a group member who is attempting to dominate the group is to challenge the behavior as it happens. Don't be hostile. Be confrontive. Here are some statements you might use:

• "Mary, we have spent a major part of the last three meetings dealing with the issue you just described. We need to focus on some other group members today."

• "Joe, our group has agreed earlier on how long we will meet. We are following the plans we made. We need to continue with the meeting."

• "Bill, I would like to get feedback from some of the others in the group about your desire to end our group meeting early again this week."

• "Chuck, I have noticed that for the last few weeks, you have brought up something very important near the time we all have agreed to end our session. Your concerns are important to you, to me, to us as a group. We want to give you the time you need, so I want to encourage you to bring this up at the beginning of our next meeting so we can give it and you the time you deserve."

Another helpful step is to get feedback from other group members. Ask group members to comment on the behavior. For example, you could ask, "James, how do you feel about Joe's request to end the meeting early today?" When you ask a question like this, ask someone who will be strong enough to give an honest response.

If the problem persists, you may need to talk to the person one to one. You may need to encourage the individual to drop out of the group to engage in one-to-one counseling sessions. Hopefully, things will not go this far, but be willing to take the necessary steps to keep any group member from dominating the group in an unhealthy way.

Before the Meeting

❏ Pray for yourself and the group members.
❏ Review the notes you took on each group member during the first meeting.
❏ Check to be sure air conditioning or heating is set properly.
❏ Be sure the room is clean with the exact number of chairs needed arranged in a circle.
❏ Have several boxes of tissue ready.
❏ Write the following discussion questions on a chalkboard or poster board:

   • Are you learning anything from working on your moral inventory that you would like to share with the group?
   • What is one area in which you have a difficult time being honest?
   • Are you engaging in self-destructive behaviors? Name them. Are you dealing with these honestly as soon as your realize you are doing them? What can you do to stop?
   • How are you doing with the compulsive behavior(s) you have chosen to work on during this group?

❏ Review the Facilitator's Self-Evaluation Checklist on page 29.

During the Meeting

1. Greet the group members as they arrive. Give out name tags.

2. Ask group members how they are doing on finding someone with whom they will share the moral inventory. Give group members who are struggling with this assignment an opportunity to express their feelings.

Some group members may express a desire to receive help in finding a listener for the moral inventory. Use some of the group time to help group members in this way.

You may find that a particular group member wants another member of the group to be his listener for the moral inventory. Help group members enforce boundaries here.

Any agreements about listening to another group member's moral inventory should be made outside the meeting. Give group members the freedom to say no if someone in the group asks them to be the listener for the moral inventory.

3. Use the following questions as a springboard for group interaction.

- Have you learned anything from working on your moral inventory that you would like to share with the group?
- What is one area in which you have a difficult time being honest?
- Are you engaging in self-destructive behaviors?
- How are you doing with the compulsive behavior(s) you have chosen to work on during this group?

Closing the Meeting

Encourage group members to complete the moral inventory and to share it with another person before the next meeting. At the same time, encourage group members to attend the next meeting whether or not they have completed the assignment. Remind them that the group exists in an atmosphere of grace.

Close the meeting with the circle of prayer. Ask each group member to thank God for something that happened during today's meeting. Close the prayer time yourself asking God to help group members with the courage needed to complete the moral inventory and to share it with someone.

After the Meeting

❏ Collect the name tags.
❏ Mark attendance on the group roster.
❏ If you are keeping a journal, record your thoughts and feelings on the meeting.
❏ Evaluate your skill-building work.

❏ Have you had a problem with one person attempting to dominate the group? If yes, how did you identify this problem? What steps did you take during today's meeting to deal with the problem?
❏ Below list three specific situations from today's meeting in which you validated a group member's feelings.

1. _____
   _____

2. _____
   _____

3. _____
   _____

❏ Mark attendance on the group roster.
❏ If you are keeping a journal, record your thoughts and feelings on the meeting.
❏ Evaluate your skill-building work. What did you say or do in this meeting to help group members develop a better understanding of God's grace? Place a check in the margin by the side of each listening skill trait you practiced during this meeting.

- When one group member is speaking, occasionally make a visual scan of the other group members. What are they saying nonverbally?
- Remember to occasionally restate and summarize what a group member has just said to the group. Then ask, "Is that what you said?" Let the group member respond.
- Remember to face the person who is speaking and to lean toward the speaker.
- When appropriate, nod your head to show you are hearing what is being said. Use an occasional verbal phrase to indicate you are listening.
- When necessary, stop the speaker and ask him or her to clarify what he or she just said.
- Make sure someone in the group gives some response when a person says something that needs a response.

❏ Evaluate the way in which you closed the meeting.

- Were you sensitive to the needs of the group as you decided when to close the meeting?

- Did you bring each issue raised to a point of closure?
- Were you sensitive to any unmet needs as you moved toward closing the meeting?
- Did you encourage group members to introduce unfinished topics at the next meeting?
- Did you stop the meeting after the circle of prayer?
- Did you permit one group member to unduly influence the time when the meeting ended?
- What did you do to communicate acceptance and concern?

CONFESSION

♦ Session Goal

Group members will discuss their progress on their moral inventories.

What to Expect

During this meeting be sensitive to four possible scenarios:

- Group members who are not making progress in completing the moral inventory. These group members need help in addressing why they have been unable to make progress on the inventory. Give them an opportunity to discuss what is holding them back. Be alert for perfectionism, fear of facing a particular issue, and fear of disclosing all to another person.
- Group members who are completing the inventory but have not found another person with whom to share it. These individuals need an opportunity to talk about sharing the inventory. Is the problem simply a matter of finding a person or scheduling a time, or is some other barrier present?
- Group members who already have completed the inventory and have found a person with whom to share it. These individuals simply will need encouragement as they prepare to share.
- You may have some group members who already have completed the inventory and have shared it. They may be ready to report on their experience.

During this meeting, attempt to affirm all group members, regardless of which of the above categories describe them and regardless of where they are in the process. Help people who seem to be stalled in finishing the inventory to articulate where their difficulties lie. Help people who are having trouble finding someone with whom to share creatively consider the names of other possible listeners.

Help individuals who already have shared the inventory but had some negative feelings about it to talk about those feelings. Give individuals who had a positive experience a chance to share those positive feelings. Their sharing can encourage others who have

not completed the assignment. You will discuss this matter more thoroughly during Session 7.

Skill Development

Work on developing skill at these activities this week:

❑ **1. Facilitate feedback (page 17).** This week give special attention to helping group members give feedback to one another. Review the section, "Facilitating Feedback," on page 17. Some examples of statements you could make to facilitate feedback within the group would be:

- "Jim, how are you feeling about what Mike said?"
- "What feelings seem to be present in our group right now?"
- "Sue, what did you feel when Lois said she felt she was getting nowhere in overcoming her food addiction?"
- "I would like about three of you to give Andy some feedback on what he has said."
- "Joe, what feelings are you reading on Gary's face?"

❑ **2. Help group members identify what they are feeling (page 18).** Identifying emotions is important in this study because compulsive behaviors often are used to mask emotional pain. During the meetings help group members to get in touch with their feelings. Help them to integrate their feelings with intellectual understanding of the issues they are dealing with. When you observe intense emotions in a particular group member, you might ask, "Do you ever engage in compulsive behavior to deal with this emotion?"

Be sensitive to your own reactions to feelings in the group. If you are feeling fear in the room, you may need to say, "I am feeling some fear right now. Is anyone else feeling fear?" Let other group members respond.

When a group member obviously is detached while others in the group are very emotionally involved, you can ask, "What are you feeling?" The person may seem perplexed at the fact that he is unable to name a feeling. He has shut down emotionally. This may feel so normal for him that he does not realize he is out of sync with the group. Ask, "Have you noticed that while everyone else in the group is deeply involved emotionally, you are not?" Through this process, you can help a group member identify the fact that he has shut down some basic emotional responses. A key element in helping group members to stay in touch with their feelings is your willingness to stay in touch with your feelings. If you refuse to allow yourself to feel your emotions, the group will follow your lead. Do not be afraid to say at various points in the meeting, "I am feeling some sadness," or "I am feeling some pain right now."

❏ **3. Stay ready for anything (page 20).** Don't try to predict or control everything that will happen in a group meeting. Some of the most significant things that will happen will not be planned and may not be clearly related to your agenda for the week. If you are a person who needs everything planned out, you will have to work on being spontaneous during the group meetings. Not knowing what will happen can produce some fear. Lean on God. Trust Him to help you no matter what happens.

❏ **4. Teach group members to help each other (page 20).** This skill begins with an attitude. The healing process for the group does not rest squarely on your shoulders. It rests in the hands of God. It also is found in the help that group members give to each other. Don't short circuit the healing of the group process by trying to do it all yourself.

Remind group members to use the phrase "I support you" or similar expressions when another group member is struggling. Encourage group members to offer a hug or some other form of encouragement when appropriate. Sometimes a group member may tell another group member something like, "You are wrong for feeling so angry." This is called "invalidating a feeling." In the group we want to be in touch with feelings. It is dangerous to deny feelings and to move straight to moral judgments. We must acknowledge our feelings and then take appropriate action to redirect our behavior. When one group member invalidates the feelings of another, focus on the group member who made the invalidating statement. Utilize the group process to help this group member discover her own issues, reflected in her attempt to suppress the feelings of another group member. You often will find that the group member who invalidates a feeling in someone else is having a fierce inner struggle with that feeling or with feelings in general. Help group members to understand why you respond to various group situations as you do. This will enable them to better help each other.

Before the Meeting

❏ Pray for yourself and group members.
❏ Check to be sure air conditioning or heating is set properly.
❏ Be sure the room is clean with the exact number of chairs needed arranged in a circle.
❏ Have several boxes of tissue ready.
❏ Write these discussion questions on a chalkboard or poster board.
  Are you making progress in completing the moral inventory? If the answer is no, can you pinpoint something specific that causes you difficulty in completing the inventory? If the answer is no, what do you need from this group to help you? If the answer is yes, share briefly with the group how this is benefiting you, and continue in your progress. We will discuss this experience further during Session 7.
❏ Review the Facilitator's Self-Evaluation Checklist on page 29.
❏ Review the notes you took on each group member during the first meeting.

During the Meeting

1. Greet the group members as they arrive. Give out name tags.
2. Ask group members to report on how their moral inventory work is progressing. Ask group members to answer the questions you wrote on the board earlier.
3. During the discussion, affirm each group member regardless of where he or she is in this process. If group members are not making progress on the inventory or have not found a person with whom to share, help them to make plans to continue. Let them know that they will have other opportunities to report to the group on this during next week's session
4. Help group members to encourage one another. Avoid a situation in which a group member feels shamed because he or she has not made progress on this assignment.
5. Report on how you are doing with the compulsive behavior(s) you have chosen to work on during this group.

Closing the Meeting

Ask group members if they are willing to let go of the failures and sins they are describing in their moral inventories. Ask them to think about this question during the week in preparation for next week's meeting when you will have a brief prayer time of letting go of past mistakes and sins.

Close the meeting with the circle of prayer. Encourage group members to ask God's help in letting go of the failures and sins of the past.

After the Meeting

❏ Collect the name tags.
❏ Mark attendance on the group roster.
❏ If you are keeping a journal, record your thoughts and feelings on the meeting.
❏ Evaluate your skill-building work.
❏ List three occasions during today's meeting when you facilitated one group member's giving feedback to another group member.

1. _____

_____

2. _____

_____

3. _____

_____

❏ List two occasions during the meeting when you helped a group member integrate emotional feelings with intellectual insights.

1. _____

_____

2. _____

_____

How much of today's meeting reflected sensitivity to emotional events? How much of today's meeting stayed on a rational level only? What part did you play in this balance?
❏ What happened during today's meeting that was totally unexpected? How did you respond to it?
❏ What did you do during this meeting to teach group members to help each other?
❏ Mark attendance on the group roster.

❏ If you are keeping a journal, record your thoughts and feelings on the meeting.
❏ Evaluate your skill-building work. What did you say or do in this meeting to help group members develop a better understanding of God's grace? Place a check in the margin by the side of each listening skill trait you practiced during this meeting.

- When one group member is speaking, occasionally make a visual scan of the other group members. What are they saying nonverbally?
- Remember to occasionally restate and summarize what a group member has just said to the group. Then ask, "Is that what you said?" Let the group member respond.
- Remember to face the person who is speaking and to lean toward the speaker.
- When appropriate, nod your head to show you are hearing what is being said. Use an occasional verbal phrase to indicate you are listening.
- When necessary, stop the speaker and ask him or her to clarify what he or she just said.
- Make sure someone in the group gives some response when a person says something that needs a response.

❏ Evaluate the way in which you closed the meeting.

- Were you sensitive to the needs of the group as you decided when to close the meeting?
- Did you bring each issue raised to a point of closure?
- Were you sensitive to any unmet needs as you moved toward closing the meeting?
- Did you encourage group members to introduce unfinished topics at the next meeting?
- Did you stop the meeting after the circle of prayer?
- Did you permit one group member to unduly influence the time when the meeting ended?
- What did you do to communicate acceptance and concern?

EMPOWERING

♦ Session Goal

Group members will discuss the results of sharing their moral inventories and will evaluate personal obstacles to receiving God's empowering for changed living.

What to Expect

During this meeting continue to be sensitive to these possible scenarios as group members report on sharing their moral inventories:

- Group members who have not completed the moral inventory. These group members need help in addressing why they have been unable to complete the inventory. Give them an opportunity to discuss what held them back. Be alert for perfectionism, fear of facing a particular issue, and fear of disclosing all to another person.
- Group members who completed the inventory but have not found another person with whom to share it. These individuals need an opportunity to talk about sharing the inventory. Is the problem simply a matter of finding a person or scheduling a time, or is some other barrier present?
- Group members who completed the inventory and shared it but who need to talk about some negative feelings they had about the experience. Perhaps the listener invalidated the group member in some way. Maybe the group member feels shame about what he or she shared. Talk about it.
- Group members who completed the moral inventory, shared it, and feel good about the experience.

If you have group members who did not complete the moral inventory or have not shared the moral inventory with another person, lovingly challenge them to continue that process. Avoid shaming or creating unnecessary pressure, but keep group members accountable. Help group members to understand that they still can complete the moral inventory during the weeks ahead.

We are now in the Upward Cycle. Recovery includes looking inward and looking outward to our relationships with others, but it also includes looking to God for strength to change and to grow. Moving beyond your past is just as crucial as is making peace with your past.

You may find that members of your group have more interest in discussing the past than in facing present compulsions and character defects. Challenge the group to the task of dealing with current issues. Talking about present compulsions may be more difficult than is talking about the past, but it is crucial to recovery.

Skill Development

Work on developing skill at these activities this week:

❑ 1. **Communicate acceptance and concern (page 16).** Review the guidelines under "Communicate Acceptance and Concern" on page 16 of this manual. You will have an excellent opportunity to practice this skill with group members who did not complete the moral inventory assignment. Work on letting these individuals know that they are not failures and that you still support them and believe in them.

Before the session think of some honest statements you can make to group members which will encourage them. Make a specific effort to use these statements during the session.

❑ 2. **Create a feeling of safety in the group and enforce boundaries (page 17).** Review the section "Create a Feeling of Safety in the Group" on page 17 of this manual. An important aspect of creating a feeling of safety in the group is enforcing boundaries during the group meetings.

Boundaries are invisible fences that surround an emotionally healthy person. We have physical boundaries. If a casual acquaintance stands three inches from your face while he or she talks with you, you will step back because this person has violated your physical boundary space. Sexual boundaries set protective limits on the sexual experiences you choose or reject. Emotional boundaries sound an alarm when someone is raging at you or attempting to control your feelings. Spiritual boundaries protect you from unhealthy forms of religion which manipulate you.

Typically your group members will deal with damaged or broken boundaries. People who have been sexually abused may have trouble understanding their right to say no to sexual advances or they may have trouble responding to appropriate touch and affection from others. People who have been physically abused may have an underdeveloped sense of the need and right to protect themselves from physical harm. An individual who grew up in a dysfunctional family may have trouble shielding himself from unnecessary emotional pain.

Your group needs to be a place where people can learn to build healthy boundaries. You can assist this process by enforcing boundaries as group members interact with one another and by respecting group members' boundaries in your interactions with them.

Encourage group members to ask permission before they give feedback to someone who has shared. Encourage them to ask permission before sharing a hug. Do not permit a group member to act in a verbally abusive way toward another group member. Do not force group members to do or say anything they are not willing to do or say. Recognize the difference between gently pushing a group member to choose to move to a point of discovery in contrast to manipulative force which pushes the individual to behavior which is against his will.

Before the Meeting

❑ Pray for yourself and group members.
❑ Check to be sure air conditioning or heating is set properly.
❑ Be sure the room is clean with the exact number of chairs needed arranged in a circle.
❑ Have several boxes of tissue ready.
❑ Write discussion questions on a chalkboard or poster board.

• Did you complete the moral inventory? If the answer is no, can you pinpoint some reasons that kept you from completing it? If the answer is no, what do you need from this group to help you? If the answer is yes, continue with the following questions.
• Did you share the moral inventory with another person?

• If the answer is yes, describe the experience.
• How did it feel?
• What did you learn from it?
• Would you like to share with the group something from your moral inventory?
• If the answer is no, can you identify some reasons that kept you from sharing the inventory with another person. Will you still attempt to share your moral inventory with someone else?
• Did the compulsive behavior you are working on in this group get worse or better as you worked on the moral inventory?

❑ Review the Facilitator's Self-Evaluation Checklist on page 29.

During the Meeting

1. Greet the group members as they arrive. Give out name tags.
2. Ask each group member to report on sharing his or her moral inventory with another person. Remember the possible scenarios:

• Group members who did not complete the moral inventory. These group members need help in addressing why they have been unable to complete the inventory.
• Group members who completed the inventory but have not shared it with another person. These individuals need an opportunity to talk about sharing the inventory. Is the problem simply a matter of finding a person or scheduling a time, or is some other barrier present?
• Group members who completed the inventory and shared it but who need to talk about some negative feelings they had about the experience.
• Group members who completed the moral inventory, shared it, and feel good about the experience.

Ask group members to answer the questions you wrote on the board earlier. During the discussion attempt to affirm all group members, regardless of which of the above categories describe them. Help people who did not complete the inventory to articulate why they have not finished it. Help people who have not shared the inventory to talk about what is happening with them. Help people who shared the inventory but had some negative feelings about it to talk about those feelings. Give people who had a positive experience a chance to share those positive feelings.

3. Use the questions below as additional discussion topics, as time permits.

> • How would you feel if Jesus wanted to wash your feet?
> • Do you have difficulty believing that things are getting better?
> • Do you serve others out of a strong self-esteem or a weak self-esteem? Do you serve others?
> • Do you feel that God's power can make a difference in your life?

Closing the Meeting

Close the meeting with the circle of prayer. Encourage group members to ask God to help them process what they learned about themselves during the moral inventory and to help them let go of the failures and sins of the past. Invite them to claim God's empowering as they pray.

After the Meeting

❑ Collect the name tags.
❑ Mark attendance on the group roster.
❑ If you are keeping a journal, record your thoughts and feelings on the meeting.
❑ Evaluate your skill-building work.
❑ List two things you did during the meeting to communicate acceptance to a group member.

1. _____

_____

2. _____

_____

❑ Do the members of your group feel that the group is a safe place? What have you done to create a feeling of safety?
❑ What did you do to help group members enforce healthy boundaries? What did you do to show respect for group members' boundaries?
❑ Mark attendance on the group roster.

❑ If you are keeping a journal, record your thoughts and feelings on the meeting.
❑ Evaluate your skill-building work. What did you say or do in this meeting to help group members develop a better understanding of God's grace? Place a check in the margin by the side of each listening skill trait you practiced during this meeting.

• When one group member is speaking, occasionally make a visual scan of the other group members. What are they saying nonverbally?
• Remember to occasionally restate and summarize what a group member has just said to the group. Then ask, "Is that what you said?" Let the group member respond.
• Remember to face the person who is speaking and to lean toward the speaker.
• When appropriate, nod your head to show you are hearing what is being said. Use an occasional verbal phrase to indicate you are listening.
• When necessary, stop the speaker and ask him or her to clarify what he or she just said.
• Make sure someone in the group gives some response when a person says something that needs a response.

❑ Evaluate the way in which you closed the meeting.

• Were you sensitive to the needs of the group as you decided when to close the meeting?
• Did you bring each issue raised to a point of closure?
• Were you sensitive to any unmet needs as you moved toward closing the meeting?
• Did you encourage group members to introduce unfinished topics at the next meeting?
• Did you stop the meeting after the circle of prayer?
• Did you permit one group member to unduly influence the time when the meeting ended?
• What did you do to communicate acceptance and concern?

Group Session 8

OPENNESS

◆ Session Goal

Each group member will evaluate how his or her experience with authority figures is affecting his or her openness to God.

What to Expect

Remember you are working on the Upward Cycle of recovery. Help group members look beyond themselves toward God. They may resist. They may want to keep looking inward without looking upward. This is a crucial juncture. This is what separates recovery from unhealthy and chronic navel gazing.

Many adult children of dysfunctional families struggle with authority-figure issues. Since God is the ultimate authority figure, this is a crucial question. Help group members relate their problems with authority figures to any difficulties they might have in being open to God's power.

Group members need to begin getting ready to complete Turning Point 6, which is a specific prayer of commitment in which the member asks God to help remove character defects. Help group members determine any barriers to completing this turning point with the past. You may find that members of your group have more interest in discussing the past than in facing present compulsions and character defects. Challenge the group to the task of dealing with current issues. Talking about present compulsions may be more difficult than is talking about the past, but it is crucial to recovery.

Skill Development

Work on developing skill at these activities this week:

❑ **1. Be personally involved without relinquishing leadership (page 16).** As facilitator, participate in the group. Be willing to share some of your own personal struggles. You need to demonstrate vulnerability. At the same time, you are the group facilitator. If you move too deeply into your own personal sharing, you suddenly may look around and discover that the group process has stopped because the group no longer has a facilitator. You face the danger of two extremes. One is being detached—assuming the role of a "professional" group facilitator. The other extreme is that of sharing at a level that deprives the group of its facilitator. Your role as group facilitator is not that of a trained expert who has solved all his problems and who shows up each week to help struggling group members with their problems. Your role is that of a fellow struggler— one who also understands emotional pain and struggles with compulsive behaviors.

❑ **2. Help group members understand psychological expression of biblical truth (page 18).** Help group members come to understand themselves within the context of the truths of the Bible. Sometimes Christians hide behind shallow recitations of biblical truth as a way of hiding from their emotional pain and from their unresolved emotional issues. The Bible does not call individuals to shallow recitations of its teachings. The God of the Bible calls people to honest self-inventory. As we better understand ourselves, we are better able to obey deep truths of Scripture.

❑ **3. Read nonverbal communication (page 19).** Review the material on reading nonverbal communication on page 19. Developing this skill is important for helping members learn to express the feelings behind the expressions on their faces or their body language.

❑ **4. Utilize good listening skills (page 20).** Listen aggressively. Much of your listening will be in the form of visual listening as you watch for nonverbal cues. Store what you hear. Some of the most effective help you will give will occur when you help a group member relate something she just said to something she said a few weeks ago.

Before the Meeting

❑ Pray for yourself and group members.
❑ Check to be sure air conditioning or heating is set properly.

❏ Be sure the room is clean with the exact number of chairs needed arranged in a circle.
❏ Have several boxes of tissue ready.
❏ Review the Facilitator's Self-Evaluation Checklist on page 29.

During the Meeting

1. Greet the group members as they arrive. Give out name tags.
2. Use the following questions as a springboard for group interaction:

- How has your experience with authority figures affected your openness to God?
- How has your experience with authority figures affected your view of the identity of God?
- Are you open and sensitive to the presence of God?
- Are you open and sensitive to the power of God?
- Are you open and sensitive to the leadership of God?
- How are you doing with the compulsive behavior(s) you have chosen to work on during this group?

Closing the Meeting

Close the meeting with the circle of prayer. Lead the group in two minutes of silent prayer. Ask each group member to seek God's presence during this time. Then, invite each group member to pray. Suggest that each ask for a greater openness to Him.

After the Meeting

❏ Collect the name tags.
❏ Mark attendance on the group roster.
❏ If you are keeping a journal, record your thoughts and feelings about the meeting.
❏ Evaluate your skill-building work.
❏ What is one thing you said in today's meeting which would indicate that you personally were involved in the meeting and were communicating some degree of vulnerability?

❏ How did you help group members integrate biblical faith with their understanding of the principles of recovery from compulsive behaviors?
❏ List three strong examples of nonverbal communication which occurred during today's meeting.

1. _____

_____

2. _____

_____

3. _____

_____

❏ List two examples of a way in which you demonstrated good listening skills during the meeting.

1. _____

_____

2. _____

_____

ASKING

♦ **Session Goal**

Each group member will have an opportunity to discuss his or her work on Turning Point 6.

What to Expect

In this session you will continue to help group members deal with the question, "Am I actually willing to let God help me change the way I think and act?" A challenge for you is that of continually bringing group members back to the spiritual side of things. Group members may want to analyze their behaviors indefinitely. Help group members to see that a time exists for facing the need to change and for asking God's help in making the necessary changes.

Skill Development

Work on developing skill at these activities this week:

❑ **1. Help group members identify what they are feeling. (page 18).** Don't let group members get stuck on purely intellectual discussions. Help group members stay in touch with their feelings. Ask, "What are you feeling right now?" "What is that feeling about?"

Stay in touch with your own feelings. Be sensitive to where you are emotionally at any given time during the meeting.

When you observe intense emotions in a particular group member, help the group member to name the emotions that are occurring. A good question to ask is, "Do you ever engage in compulsive behavior to deal with this emotion?"

Sometimes a certain emotion will hang over the group like a cloud. When you have a sense of such a powerful emotion occurring in the group, this may signal that the entire group is feeling something but refusing to

acknowledge it. Or, it simply may be a powerful feeling that most of the people in the group are experiencing at the same time. In either case, call that emotion by name. "I'm feeling a lot of (name the feeling) in the room," you can say. Ask group members if they sense the same feeling. Ask, "What is this (name the feeling) about?" Discuss the origin of the emotion that hangs over the group.

❑ **2. Validate feelings (page 20).** Adult children are people who received negative messages about their own feelings. In the family of origin some feelings were not OK. Perhaps some feelings were OK for other family members but not for the adult child. Maybe the adult child was not allowed to feel much of anything.

Make your group a safe place for people to express and acknowledge emotions. Stay away from labeling certain emotions as "bad." Emphasize that we need to acknowledge feelings which exist inside us. Say, "In this group it is OK for you to experience your emotions."

Remind the group about the importance of boundaries in the expression of emotions. For example, people need to express anger, but hitting someone because you are angry is not appropriate.

Before the Meeting

❑ Pray for yourself and group members.
❑ Check to be sure air conditioning or heating is set properly.
❑ Be sure the room is clean with the exact number of chairs needed arranged in a circle.
❑ Have several boxes of tissue ready.
❑ Review the Facilitator's Self-Evaluation Checklist on page 29.

During the Meeting

1. Greet the group members as they arrive. Give out name tags.

2. Use the following questions as a springboard for group interaction:

> - Did you complete your list of character flaws? If not, what stopped you?
> - Did you write a prayer asking God to remove your character flaws? If no, can you identify some things that caused you to have difficulty writing this prayer?
> - How did this process feel to you?
> - How are you doing with the compulsive behavior(s) you have chosen to work on during this group?

Closing the Meeting

1. Encourage any group member who has not completed the moral inventory and shared it with another person to work on it during the week ahead. Encourage members to complete the inventory even if they feel they now are behind the rest of the group. Encourage them that they can still benefit from completing the inventory.
2. Encourage any group member who has not completed Turning Point 6 to work on it during the week ahead.
3. Close the meeting with the circle of prayer.

After the Meeting

❏ Collect the name tags.
❏ Mark attendance on the group roster.
❏ If you are keeping a journal, record your thoughts and feelings about the meeting.
❏ Evaluate your skill-building work.
  - Did this meeting deal with emotional and intellectual issues or simply with emotional issues? What impact did your leadership have?
  - Did the meeting feel like a safe environment in which group members could express their emotions? What factors seemed to make it feel safe? What impact did your leadership have?

INTIMACY

♦ Session Goal

Each group member will explore his or her feelings about emotional intimacy.

What to Expect

Today's meeting presents a shift from the introspective focus of the Inward Cycle and the spiritual focus of the Upward Cycle to the relational focus of the Outward Cycle.

Dysfunctional families do not foster the development of interpersonal relational skills. Adult children of dysfunctional families often are lonely people because they have trouble being close to others.

During this meeting you will help group members understand what intimacy is. You will identify some of the factors that make intimacy difficult for adult children from dysfunctional families. And, you will underscore the importance of honesty as the foundation for intimate relationships. An important issue for some group members will be, "Do I want emotionally intimate relationships?" Group members may need help in moving beyond a fear of intimate relationships.

Skill Development

Work on developing skill at this activity this week:

❑ **Be willing to confront in love (page 16).** Sometimes love is tough. Sometimes caring for a person means being willing to say something that he or she does not want to hear. Confrontation motivated by love is sensitive to timing and wording. It is not hostile or destructive. It is sensitive to how much the individual can deal with at the time of the confrontation.

Be sensitive to the fact that some of the people in your group may never be as open as they are now to your constructive confrontation.

If you feel that you must smooth over or ignore every conflict, you will have trouble facilitating this group. Conflict is not always bad. Confrontation can lead to understanding and healing.

Before the Meeting

❑ Pray for yourself and group members.
❑ Check to be sure air conditioning or heating is set properly.
❑ Be sure the room is clean with the exact number of chairs needed arranged in a circle.
❑ Have several boxes of tissue ready.
❑ Review the Facilitator's Self-Evaluation Checklist on page 29.

During the Meeting

1. Greet the group members as they arrive. Give out name tags.
2. Use the following questions as a springboard for group interaction:

> • What is emotional intimacy?
> • Is emotional intimacy difficult for you? Can you pinpoint reasons why it is difficult for you?
> • What substitutes for emotional intimacy have you chosen?
> • Do you believe God can help you find emotional intimacy?
> • How are you doing with the compulsive behavior(s) you have chosen to work on during this group?

Closing the Meeting

1. Ask your group members how they feel about the fact that the group soon will be ending. You may find

that the members of your group feel sad and concerned about the group's disbanding in a few weeks. Here are some suggestions which can help.

• Help group members process the grief they feel about the group's ending. Help them to talk about their feelings.
• Some group members may choose to participate in a second Heart-to-Heart group. Individuals remain in denial well into the life of the group but who begin to discover significant insights near the end of the group's life will be good candidates for a repeat group.
• Another option is to discuss the possibility of this same group continuing for another 13-week period. The group could continue as a weekly support group. You might consider shared or rotating leadership. Group members may participate in other LIFE® Support Group Series or LIFE courses offered by your church. See pages 203-204 of the *Moving Beyond Your Past* member's book for suggestions for persons who desire additional growth.

Whatever decision the group makes about an ongoing focus, make sure the group has a clearly stated purpose, a covenant, and a pre-defined life span. A group benefits if it re-evaluates its purpose and direction about once a quarter. If the group is interested in continuing, gather preliminary input from the group and plan to discuss the group's future more fully during the last meeting.

2. Close the meeting with the circle of prayer. Encourage each group member to thank God for something that happened during today's meeting.

After the Meeting

❑ Collect the name tags.
❑ Mark attendance on the group roster.
❑ If you are keeping a journal, record your thoughts and feelings about the meeting.
❑ Evaluate your skill-building work.
  • Describe an incident from today's meeting or from a recent meeting in which you lovingly confronted a group member. What was the group member's response? What did you learn from this experience?

VULNERABILITY

◆ **Session Goal**

Each group member will examine his or her willingness to be vulnerable in relationships and will make a list of people he or she has wronged.

What to Expect

Being vulnerable in relationships is one of the toughest challenges for adult children of dysfunctional families. In this unit group members will explore the meaning of vulnerability as well as factors which make becoming vulnerable difficult for them.

We will discuss the importance of boundaries. We will challenge group members to make a reconciliation list which includes any relationships with unresolved hurts which the group member initiated.

Skill Development

Work on developing skill at these activities this week:

❑ **1. Communicate acceptance and concern (page 16).** This week's meeting offers a powerful opportunity to communicate unconditional acceptance within the group. Since group members will be confronting relational problems they have initiated, you will have a special opportunity to communicate acceptance and concern.

Remember that accepting a person as he is does not necessarily mean you agree with that person's values or choices. It does mean that you are willing to love this person now without waiting for certain conditions to be met.

Remember the destructive power of shame in the lives of the members of your group. Hopefully, members of your group have won major victories over shame. However, shame-based identities do not vanish overnight. Be alert to opportunities to cut through shame and to affirm people in your group.

❑ **2. Teach group members to help each other (page 20).** Throughout the meeting, work on letting go of the group. Give the group members an extra moment or two to say what you would have said. You may be tempted to make the first comment after someone shares, but train yourself to withhold jumping in with your comments immediately to enable group members to affirm or reflect with the person who has just shared. As much as possible, let the group members help each other with a minimum of intervention from you.

Before the Meeting

❑ Pray for yourself and group members.
❑ Check to be sure air conditioning or heating is set properly.
❑ Be sure the room is clean with the exact number of chairs needed arranged in a circle.
❑ Have several boxes of tissue ready.
❑ Review the Facilitator's Self-Evaluation Checklist on page 29.

During the Meeting

1. Greet the group members as they arrive. Give out name tags.
2. Use the following questions as a springboard for group interaction:

- Is vulnerability difficult for you? Can you name some reasons that cause it to be difficult?
- Do you feel that vulnerability is the same as being a doormat or being weak? What is the difference?
- Is it difficult for you to admit mistakes to others? Can you pinpoint some things that cause this to be difficult for you?
- How did you do in preparing your reconciliation list? Talk about the experience.
- How are you doing with the compulsive behavior(s) you have chosen to work on during this group?

Closing the Meeting

Close the meeting with the circle of prayer. Encourage each group member to thank God for something that happened during today's meeting.

After the Meeting

❑ Collect the name tags.
❑ Mark attendance on the group roster.
❑ If you are keeping a journal, record your thoughts and feelings about the meeting.
❑ Evaluate your skill-building work.

- What did you do during this meeting to communicate acceptance and concern?
- What did you do to help group members learn to help each other?

SHARING

◆ **Session Goal**

Group members will report on their progress in completing the work of contacting persons they listed on their reconciliation worksheets.

What to Expect

Some group members will be eager to share reports on contacts they have made for reconciliation. Some will have positive reports. Allow them to share the joy and cleansing they feel. Others will have received mixed messages. Help them probe the questions they have about their contacts. Still others may have had negative contacts. Help group members who had negative experiences process their thoughts and feelings.

Some group members will have avoided the assignment. Remember that each group member participates voluntarily, but encourage the group member to talk about why he or she has not acted on the assignment. Help the group member to understand that he or she can carry out the assignment after this meeting.

Before the Meeting

❑ Pray for yourself and group members.
❑ Check to be sure air conditioning or heating is set properly.
❑ Be sure the room is clean with the exact number of chairs needed arranged in a circle.
❑ Have several boxes of tissue ready.
❑ Review the Facilitator's Self-Evaluation Checklist on page 29.

During the Meeting

1. Greet the group members as they arrive. Give out name tags.
2. Begin by inviting group members to report on the results of their reconciliation contacts. If time permits

use the following discussion questions for further interaction:

- Do you have problems with jealousy?
- Do these problems have roots in your past?
- Do you do things for other people in order to get what you want? Can you identify some reasons that you take these actions?
- How are you doing with the compulsive behavior(s) you have chosen to work on during this group?

Closing the Meeting

One option for further group work is that of offering this group again and studying the same material in another 13-week format. If you are considering offering this group the option of continuing for another 13-week period, allow some time at the end of the meeting to discuss the next phase of the group.

Be careful to build the meeting around the discussion suggested under "During the Meeting." Discussing the group's future plans should not be the main event of this meeting.

When you are ready to address the group's future plans, discuss the following:

1. Who will lead the group?
   - A selected facilitator?
   - Leadership rotation among group members?
2. When and where will the group meet? When will the next meeting be?
3. How often will the group meet?
4. What will be the purpose of the group?
5. Will you use the same covenant you used for this group? If not, what covenant will you use?
6. Will the group use a particular book or other study material?
7. When will the new group evaluate its plans beyond the next 13 weeks?

Refer to the suggestions on pages 203-204 of the member's book to help members who want further opportunities for spiritual growth. If you run out of time for this discussion, the new group can use its first meeting to complete plans for its next phase of meetings.

Close the meeting with the circle of prayer. Encourage each group member to thank God for the group experience.

After the Meeting

❑ Collect the name tags.
❑ Mark attendance on the group roster.
❑ If you are keeping a journal, record your thoughts and feelings about the meeting.

RECYCLING

♦ Session Goal

Group members will review the progress they have made in the group and will share a personal plan for continuing in the cycles of recovery

What to Expect

Expect some joy and a sense of "I have found help; I am getting better" as group members reflect on the progress they have made in the group.

Expect some sadness and even fear as group members think about the group's coming to an end. The sadness is about ending what has been a positive experience of emotional intimacy. The fear may be about regressing back to earlier patterns of emotional dysfunction once the group disbands.

Expect some affirmation as you hear group members talk about the progress they have made.

During this session you will help group members think in a positive way about continuing in the recovery process. You will underscore the importance of having a plan for ongoing spiritual and emotional growth.

Before the Meeting

❏ Pray for yourself and group members.
❏ Check to be sure air conditioning or heating is set properly.
❏ Be sure the room is clean with the exact number of chairs needed arranged in a circle.
❏ Have several boxes of tissue ready.
❏ Review the notes you took during the first meeting. Bring the notes with you to the meeting.
❏ Review the Facilitator's Self-Evaluation Checklist on page 29.

During the Meeting

1. Greet the group members as they arrive. Give out name tags.
2. Use the following discussion questions for further interaction:

- What goals have you accomplished during the last 12 weeks?
- What are some ways your thinking has changed during the group?
- How would you express your gratitude for these changes?
- What are some important areas of your life which need constant monitoring?
- What is a brief summary of your self-care plan? Share it with the group.

Allow each group member to share his or her responses to all these questions before you proceed to the next group member. As each person shares, glance at the notes you made during the first meeting. Help individuals remember the three statements each shared during the first meeting describing goals for life in a state of spiritual and emotional health. Be ready to affirm each group member by making personal comments about positive changes you have seen. Some group members may not realize what they have accomplished. Help them to see and to acknowledge the progress they have made.

After all the members of the group have shared their responses to the five questions, ask each group member to share a summary of his or her plan for continuing recovery. Encourage and commend each person. Make helpful suggestions.

Closing the Meeting

1. If you plan to offer this group the option of continuing for another 13-week period, allow some time at the end of the meeting to discuss the next phase

of the group. Be careful to build the meeting around the discussion suggested under "During the Meeting." Do not make discussing the group's future plans the main event of this meeting.

2. When you are ready to address the group's future plans, discuss the following:

- Who will lead the group?
  a. A selected facilitator?
  b. Rotating leadership among group members?
- When and where will the group meet? When will the next meeting be?
- How often will the group meet?
- What will be the purpose of the group?
- Will you use the same set of agreements you used for this group? If not, what agreements will you use?
- Will the group use a particular book or other study material? (Remember the suggestions for further study that appear on pages of the member's book.)
- When will the new group evaluate its plans beyond the next 13 weeks?

If you run out of time for this discussion, the new group can use its first meeting of the next 13 meetings to complete plans for its next phase of meetings.

Close the meeting with the circle of prayer. Encourage each group member to thank God for the group experience.

After the Meeting

❏ Mark attendance on the group roster.
❏ If you are keeping a journal, record your thoughts and feelings about the meeting.